THE BOSPHORUS

by

JOHN FREELY

Black and white photographs
by Anthony E. Baker

Published by the Redhouse Press,
Rızapaşa Yokuşu No. 50, Mercan, Istanbul

© 1993 Redhouse Press
Cover photos: Ara Güler
Cover design: Cerina Logico Blakney
Index: Charles P. Blakney
Maps and glossary: Redhouse Press

ISBN 975-413-062-0

Printed in Turkey by Uycan Yayınları Anonim Şirketi,
Büyükdere Caddesi No. 53, Maslak, Istanbul

IN MEMORY OF HILARY SUMNER-BOYD

CONTENTS

List of Illustrations		*VIII*
Maps		*X*
Introduction		*XIII*
Bibliographic Note		*XIV*
Glossary of Turkish Terms		*XV*
Chapter 1	The Bosphorus and the City	*1*
Chapter 2	The Galata Bridge to Kabataş	*11*
Chapter 3	Kabataş to Bebek	*34*
Chapter 4	Bebek to Rumelihisarı	*55*
Chapter 5	Rumelihisarı to Rumelikavağı	*72*
Chapter 6	The Upper Bosphorus	*93*
Chapter 7	Anadolukavağı to Anadoluhisarı	*105*
Chapter 8	Anadoluhisarı to Üsküdar	*120*
Chapter 9	Üsküdar	*142*
Chapter 10	A Café on the Bosphorus	*163*
Index		*171*

LIST OF ILLUSTRATIONS

The photographs listed below in italics are from *The Beauties of the Bosphorus* (1838) by Julia Pardoe.

1. *The Bosphorus, from above Beshik-Tash, looking north* p. XVI
2. *Entrance to the Black Sea, from the Giant's Grave* p. XVI
3. Eminönü: İskeles with the Topkapı Sarayı in the background and the Sepetçiler Kasrı (left) p. 12
4. The Haghia Sophia (left) and the Topkapı Sarayı (center) p. 12
5. *The Port of Constantinople* p. 14
6. *Mosque of Sultana Valide, from the Port* p. 14
7. *The Tower of Galata* p. 16
8. Galata: The Galata Tower with the Customs House in the foreground p. 16
9. Cihangir: Cihangir Camii p. 31
10. Fındıklı: Molla Çelebi Camii p. 31
11. Dolmabahçe: Dolmabahçe Camii p. 33
12. *Dolma-Batche, from the Necropolis of Pera* p. 36
13. Dolmabahçe: Dolmabahçe Sarayı p. 36
14. Ortaköy: Mecidiye Camii with the Boğaziçi Köprüsü in the background p. 50
15. Arnavutköy: Arnavutköy İskelesi prior to the new coast road's construction p. 50
16. Bebek: Bebek Camii p. 53
17. Bebek: Egyptian Consulate p. 54
18. Bebek: A Bosphorus view from above Bebek p. 54
19. *Bebec on the Bosphorus* p. 56
20. *Turkish Country House on the Bosphorus* p. 56
21. *The Castles of Europe and Asia* p. 61
22. Rumelihisarı p. 61

23. Rumelihisarı: Hacı Kemalettin Camii p. 64
24. Fatih Sultan Mehmet Köprüsü p. 71
25. Baltalimanı: *Yalıs* above the coast road p. 73
26. Emirgân: Şerifler Yalısı p. 73
27. Emirgân: View of the *çeşme* from the mosque p. 75
28. İstinye p. 77
29. Yeniköy: *Yalıs* p. 77
30. *Istenia, near Therapia* p. 81
31. *Therapia, and the Giant's Grave* p. 81
32. Büyükdere: Sadberk Hanım Müzesi p. 87
33. *Fort Biel-Gorod* p. 95
34. *The Bosphorus, opposite the Genoese Castle* p. 95
35. Rumelifeneri: Harbor of the "Clashing Rocks" p. 103
36. Genoese Castle above Anadolukavağı p. 103
37. Hekimbaşı Salih Efendi Yalısı p. 114
38. Amcazade Hüseyin Paşa Yalısı p.114
39. Anadoluhisarı p. 122
40. *Fountain near the Asian Valley of Sweet Waters, on the Bosphorus* p.122
41. *Musicians at the Asian Valley of Sweet Waters* p. 124
42. Küçüksu: Küçüksu Kasrı p. 124
43. Küçüksu: Valide Sultan Mihrişah Çeşmesi p. 127
44. Kıbrıslı Yalısı p. 129
45. Ostrorog Yalısı p. 129
46. Kandilli: *Yalıs* p. 134
47. Kuleli: Kuleli Naval Officer's Training College p. 134
48. Beylerbeyi: Beylerbeyi Camii p. 137
49. Beylerbeyi: Beylerbeyi Sarayı p. 137
50. Üsküdar: İskele Camii p. 145
51. Üsküdar: Şemsi Paşa Camii p. 145
52. *The Guz-Couli or Maiden's Tower* p. 149
53. Kız Kulesi p. 149
54. *Constantinople from Scutari* p. 151
55. *View from the Ferry at Scutari* p. 151

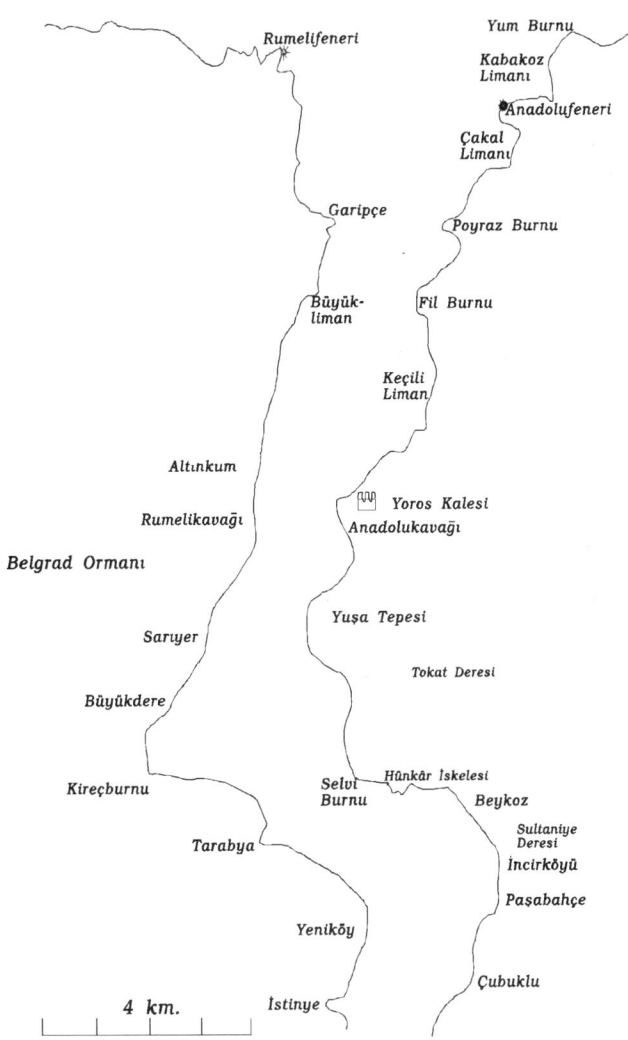

INTRODUCTION

This is a book about the Bosphorus, the strait in northwestern Turkey that separates Europe from Asia between the Black Sea and the Sea of Marmara. The chapters that follow will describe the Bosphorus and its shores, beginning with an introduction to the topography, mythology and history of the strait and its tributary, the Golden Horn, particularly as they relate to the development of the imperial city at its southern end. Subsequent chapters will take us up the European shore of the strait from the Golden Horn to the Black Sea, and then back down the Asian side to the Sea of Marmara. En route the book will describe the historic monuments on the Bosphorus, along with the succession of seaside villages that are strung out along both shores of the strait, some of them as old as the city itself. Along the way we will be constantly looking at the Bosphorus and its shores, its flora and fauna, its fish and fishermen and boatmen, its currents and the lore of its winds, its seasons and its moods, reflecting on the profound influence it has on the appearance and character of Istanbul, its ageless beauty in the background of every view of the imperial city that it brought into being twenty-seven or more centuries ago.

A BIBLIOGRAPHICAL NOTE

The Bosphorus has been at the centre of human events since the beginning of recorded history, and before that it figures prominently in the first exploration myths of the Greeks. Despite this very few books have been written about the Bosphorus, none of them in English, and none in any language after the nineteenth century.

The earliest book on the Bosphorus is by the French scholar Pierre Gilles (1490-1555), whose name is better known as the Latinized Petrus Gyllius. Gyllius spent the years 1544-47 and 1550 in Istanbul studying the antiquities of the city and its environs, particularly the Bosphorus. He worked for the remaining five years of his life in Rome writing up his researches, but he died before completing them, on 5 January 1555. The task was carried through to completion by his nephew Antoine Gilles, who at Lyon in 1561 published Gyllius' *Four Books on the Topography of Constantinople and On its Antiquities*, and his *Three Books on the Thracian Bosphorus*, all in Latin. Gyllius' work on the Antiquities of Constantinople was translated into English by John Ball in 1729, and an excellent modern edition of this was published in 1988 by Ronald G. Musto. But Gyllius' work on the Bosphorus has never been published in English or any other modern language, except for a number of passages translated by Hilary Sumner-Boyd for our *Strolling Through Istanbul*, first published by Redhouse Press in 1972. These passages appear in the chapter on the Bosphorus in *Strolling Through Istanbul*, which is the primary source for the present book, whose debt to the work of Hilary Sumner-Boyd is only inadequately expressed in the dedication.

GLOSSARY OF TURKISH TERMS

avlu	courtyard
ayazma	spring of water regarded as sacred
bedesten	covered market
cami	mosque
camekân	dressing room of a Turkish bath
çeşme	fountain
dalyan	fishgarth
dershane	lecture hall
göbektaşı	heated marble platform on which one lies to sweat in a Turkish bath
hamam	public bath, Turkish bath
hararet	the hot room in a *hamam* which contains the *göbektaşı*
harem	woman's quarters
imaret	soup kitchen for the poor
iskele	ferryboat landing
köprü	bridge
Kuran kürsüsü	(raised throne-like) chair (from which an *imam* preaches)
külliye	complex of buildings adjacent to a mosque
medrese	madrasah (theological school attached to a mosque)
meydan	public square
mihrap	mihrab (niche in a mosque wall indicating the direction of Mecca)
mimber	minbar (pulpit beside the *mihrap* reached by a long, straight flight of steps
namazgâh	open-air prayer place (usually an unroofed stone platform)
pazar kayığı	large, heavy rowboat carrying passengers and freight to the villages on the Bosphorus
salon	large room
sebil	kiosk built for the distribution of free drinking water
selamlık	the part of a large Muslim house reserved for men
semahane	building where Mevlevi dervishes perform their whirling dance
şadırvan	fountain (used for ritual ablutions and usually situated in the middle of a mosque courtyard)
şerefe	balcony (surrounding a minaret)
tekke	dervish lodge
türbe	(large, usually domed) tomb, turbeh.

The Bosphorus, from above Beshik-Tash, looking north

Entrance to the Black Sea, from the Giant's Grave

CHAPTER ONE
THE BOSPHORUS AND THE CITY

According to Petrus Gyllius, the Bosphorus is the "Strait that surpasses all straits, because with one key it opens and closes two worlds, two seas." The two worlds to which Gyllius refers are Europe and Asia, and the two seas are the Marmara and the Black Sea, which he calls by their ancient Greek names, the Propontis and the Pontus Euxinos, or Euxine. And the key to these two worlds and their interconnected land-locked seas is Istanbul, the only city in the world that stands astride two continents. This is the imperial city that for sixteen centuries was the capital in turn of the Byzantine and Ottoman Empires, known to the Greeks as Constantinople, the ancient Byzantium. For this city commands the southern approach to the Bosphorus, which separates Europe and Asia at a place that has been the focus of the major land-routes between the two continents since the beginning of recorded history. The missing link in this intercontinental route was filled in with the completion of a bridge across the Bosphorus between Ortaköy and Beylerbeyi in 1973, on the fiftieth anniversary of the founding of the Turkish Republic. The link was strengthened by the opening in 1988 of a second bridge, between Rumelihisarı and Anadoluhisarı. The latter span was erected at the same place where Mandrocles of Samos built a pontoon bridge 2,500 years previously, in 512 BC, so that the Persian King Darius could march his army from Asia to Europe at the outset of his campaign against the Scythians. The building of this bridge is mentioned by Herodotus in his *Histories,* the earliest historic reference to both the Bosphorus and the city of Byzantium, which was then already halfway through the second century of its existence.

Any description of the Bosphorus involves the name Rumeli and Anadolu, for the first of these is used in referring to places on

2 THE BOSPHORUS AND THE CITY

the European side of the strait and the second to those on the Asian shore. The first of these toponyms derives from that of the old Ottoman province of Rumeli, which included Thrace and southern Bulgaria. This name comes from the Turkish *Rum*, or Rome, referring to the eastern Roman dominions that later came to be called the Byzantine Empire. Anadolu is the Turkish for Anatolia, the Asian part of Turkey, where ninety-seven percent of the country's land-mass is located. Anatolia is the Greek word for "east", more literally the 'land of sunrise'. The name Asia may originally have had the same meaning as this in both the Indo-European and Semitic families of languages, while Europe may have meant "sunset", or the "land of darkness". The distinction between these two names would have been dramatically evident to ancient navigators making their way up the Bosphorus from the Propontis to the Euxine, with Asia to the east and Europe to the west, the sun rising above one shore of the strait and then setting below the other, the deep waters of the channel clearly dividing the "land of sunrise" from the "land of darkness."

The Bosphorus changes direction half-a-dozen times as it flows from the Black Sea to the Marmara. Its maximum width is three and one-half kilometers, measured along a line between Rumelifeneri and Anadolufeneri, the Lighthouses of Europe and Asia, which mark the entrance to the strait from the Black Sea. From there the strait runs in the approximate direction northeast to southwest for the first ten kilometers of its course, converging to a width ranging from 1200-1500 meters about two-thirds of the way along this stretch. After this first ten kilometers the Bosphorus abruptly changes course, flowing from northwest to southeast for the next ten kilometers, and then for the next three kilometers beyond that it changes direction to flow northeast to southwest. This brings it to the Narrows, where it flows from north to south for three kilometers, with the facing continental shores only 700 meters apart between Rumelihisarı and Anadoluhisarı, the Castles of Europe and Asia. At the southern end of the Narrows the Bosphorus is fed on its Anatolian side by two streams known as

THE BOSPHORUS AND THE CITY 3

the Sweet Waters of Asia, in Turkish called Göksu and Küçüksu. Beyond the Narrows the strait widens gradually as it follows an undulating course in the general direction northeast to southwest for the next nine kilometers.

The average depth of the Bosphorus at the center of its channel is about 50 to 75 meters, but at one point just below the southern end of the Narrows it reaches a depth of 110 meters. The predominant surface current flows at a rate of two to four knots from the Black Sea to the Marmara, but, because of the sinuosity of the channel, eddies producing strong reverse currents flow around most of the indentations of the shore. A very strong wind from the south, the dreaded Lodos, may reverse the main current and make it flow toward the Black Sea, in which case the counter-eddies may also change their direction. At a depth of about 40 meters there is a sub-surface current, called *kanal* in Turkish, which flows from the Marmara to the Black Sea. The *kanal* is for the most part prevented from entering the Black Sea by a threshold just beyond the mouth of the Bosphorus. This subterranean ledge turns back the lower current, which is denser and more saline than the main layer above, and forces it to merge with the upper stream, so that its waters are ultimately driven back to the Marmara by the surface current. The *kanal* is strong enough so that under certain conditions, if fishing nets are lowered into it, it can pull boats toward the Black Sea against the surface current.

There are several theories concerning the origin of the Bosphorus, with most scholars agreed that it dates from the fairly recent geological past. One theory is that the Bosphorus was worn away as an exit channel for the waters of the Black Sea, which was originally a lake, and that this inundated the lower and more level terrain now covered by the Sea of Marmara, which in turn wore an outgoing channel to the Aegean through the Dardanelles, the Greek Hellespont. Another theory holds that the Bosphorus was formed in a cataclysmic sundering of the earth's surface to produce this deep and jagged cleft between the European and Asian continents, with the waters of the Black Sea then suddenly pour-

4   THE BOSPHORUS AND THE CITY

ing through in one gigantic tidal wave that has continued undiminished ever since. A layman would tend to agree with the latter and more dramatic theory, for the opposing continental shores appear as if they once fitted into one another like the pieces in a jig-saw puzzle before they were forced apart in a primeval earthquake, whose geological scars seem only recently healed and covered over by the greenery that still adorns the hills and valleys along the straits outside the sprawling urban mass of Istanbul. Both shores of the Bosphorus are indented by frequent bays and harbors, and in general it will be found that an indentation in one shore corresponds to a promontory on the other side of the strait. Most of the bays are in the mouths of valleys reaching back into the hills on either side of the strait, and a great many of these declivities have streams that flow into the Bosphorus. Almost all of these are insignificant, with only the Sweet Waters of Asia having any claim to be called rivers, and even there both Göksu and Küçüksu are quite small. Both shores are lined with hills, none of them very high, the most imposing being Büyük Çamlıca (262 meters) and Yuşa Tepesi (201 meters), both on the Asian side; nevertheless, particularly on the upper Bosphorus, the hills often seem much higher than they really are because of the way in which they plunge down in precipitous cliffs into the sea. Despite the rapidly growing urbanization of the Bosphorus shores, they are still well-wooded, especially with cypresses, umbrella-pines, plane-trees, horse-chestnuts, terebinths and judas trees. The magenta to pink blossoms of the judas trees in spring, mingled with the mauve flowers of the ubiquitous wisteria and the red and white candles of the chestnuts, make the Bosphorus surpassingly beautiful in that season, painfully so in late April, when nightingales begin serenading one another in the blossoming hills and valleys along the strait.

The casual visitor to Istanbul, particularly if one comes in summer, might find it difficult to believe that the Bosphorus can be a perverse and dangerous body of water. Seen from the hills along its shores as it curves and widens and narrows, it often looks

THE BOSPHORUS AND THE CITY 5

like a long lake or a series of lakes, while its rapid flow from the Black Sea to the Sea of Marmara gives it somewhat the character and appearance of a great river. Yet anyone who has observed its erratic currents and counter-currents, its various winds that encourage or hinder navigation, the impenetrable fogs that envelop it, even occasionally the icebergs that choke it, will realize that it is indeed part of the ungovernable sea. Here Belisarius fought the invincible whale Porphyry, that Moby Dick who wrecked all shipping on the Bosphorus for months; and here Gyllius observed the largest shark he had ever seen. And on halcyon days in mid-winter schools of dolphins can be seen frolicking in its waters as they make their way through the strait. Since it is an international waterway, the Bosphorus is busy day and night with a heavy traffic of oil tankers and cargo ships, as well as occasional ocean liners and war ships, along with the colorful ferryboats that flit back and forth between the continents on their way up and down the strait. The numerous sharp and unexpected bends in the strait, along with the occasional storms and dense fogs, can make the passage quite difficult at times. Nearly every year large ships collide with one another on the Bosphorus or run aground on its banks, smashing into houses or roadways along its shores. Those who have grown old along the Bosphorus tell stories of being awakened from their slumbers by a terrific crash, to find their front parlor in ruins and the rusty prow of a tramp steamer protruding into the library, or of how a quiet supper was suddenly disrupted when the yard-arm of a passing schooner smashed through the dining room window and swept the table clear.

Just before the Bosphorus reaches the Marmara it is joined on its European side by the Golden Horn, a scimitar-shaped inlet that is fed at its upper end by two streams called the Sweet Waters of Europe, known in Turkish as Alibey Suyu and Kâğıthane Suyu. The Horn, known to the Greeks as Chryso Keras, is some eight kilometers in length from its source to the point where it enters the Bosphorus. Over the last five kilometers of its course the Golden Horn divides the European side of the city into two

6   THE BOSPHORUS AND THE CITY

parts, of which the most ancient is on the south bank. This is the old city that some prefer to call Stamboul, the former Constantinople. The names Stamboul and Istanbul are corruptions of the Greek *stin poli,* meaning "in the city", or "to the city", referring to Constantinople, "the City" beyond compare.

Stamboul comprises a more or less triangular promontory that forms the southeasternmost extension of the European continent, bounded on the north by the Golden Horn, on the south by the Marmara, and on the west by the ancient fortifications of Byzantine Constantinople, the Theodosian walls. These walls enclose seven hills, six of them rising from the ridge that parallels the Golden Horn, the seventh with its double summit in the southwestern part of the city, where it slopes down to the Marmara shore. The apex of this triangle is a promontory known in Turkish as Sarayburnu, or Palace Point, which juts into the middle of the strait where the Golden Horn joins the Bosphorus. The promontory takes its name from the Turkish palace of Topkapı Sarayı, which for four centuries was the imperial residence of the Ottoman sultans, its domed pavilions and walled gardens still adorning the acropolis above Sarayburnu, which Gyllius numbered first among the seven hills of the ancient city. The Great Palace of Byzantium also stood on the First Hill, but this fabled pleasure-dome has now all but vanished save for one ruined facade, the rest buried under Ottoman edifices and modern Turkish houses. Thus Istanbul is a veritable palimpsest of empires, the ruins of successive civilizations buried under the remains of those that have succeeded them in turn. And nowhere is this more evident than on the acropolis at the confluence of the Bosphorus and the Golden Horn, for this is where the ancient Greek colony of Byzantium was founded just before the dawn of recorded history, the story of its foundation shrouded in the mists of Bosphorean legend.

The earliest Greek myths about the Bosphorus probably date from the end of the Bronze Age, the latter part of the second millennium BC, when the Hellenes first came in contact with the world beyond the Aegean end of the Mediterranean. One of these

THE BOSPHORUS AND THE CITY

myths tells the story of Zeus and his mistress Io, daughter of the river-god Inachus, whom he changed into a heifer to conceal her from his jealous wife Hera. But Hera was not deceived and drove Io away, pursuing her with a relentless gadfly that forced her to swim across the northernmost of the two straits separating Europe from Asia. Thenceforth this strait bore the name Bosphorus, or Ford of the Cow, commemorating the flight of Io, the "Inachean daughter, beloved of Zeus." Another version of the myth has it that before Io crossed the strait she bore Zeus a daughter, the nymph Keroessa, who was born on the upper reaches of the Golden Horn at a place called Semistra. Keroessa in turn became the mistress of Poseidon and gave birth to Byzas, the Thracian hero who became the eponymous founder of Byzantium, a legend that takes one forward centuries in time to the pre-dawn of the historic era.

The first Greek exploration of the straits leading from the Aegean to the Euxine probably took place toward the end of the Bronze Age, and the Trojan War described in Homer's *Iliad* may be based on an actual campaign in this eastward Hellenic expansion into Anatolia. The legend of Jason and his search for the Golden Fleece is perhaps a folk-memory of these early Greek voyages through the straits, which expanded the bounds of their known world. Homer placed Jason's voyage a generation before the Trojan War, which both ancient and modern scholars have dated to c. 1200 BC. When Jason decided to set off on his expedition he commissioned a ship called Argo, in whose bow Athena inserted a piece of wood from the oracular oak at Dodona, giving it the power of speech. After the launching of Argo, whose name means "swift," heroes from all over the Greek world volunteered to fill the fifty seats on its rowing benches, including Orpheus and Heracles. These were the Argonauts, the crew of the vessel that Spenser in the *Faery Queene* called "the wondred Argo, which first through the Euxine Sea bore all the flower of Greece." The only full account of the voyage of Argo that has survived is the *Argonautica* of Apollonius of Rhodes, written in the mid-third century BC. But Jason and the Argonauts are mentioned by sources

8 THE BOSPHORUS AND THE CITY

as early as Homer, who in the Odyssey has Odysseus speak of "...Argo, who is in all men's minds." Pindar refers to the Argonauts in one of his *Pythian Odes,* where he writes of how "Hera kindled sweet desire in the sons of God for the ship Argo. So that none should be left behind to nurse a life without danger at his mother's side, but rather that he should find even against death the fairest antidote in his own courage along with the others of his age."

Gyllius identified a number of sites along the Bosphorus associated with the legend of Jason and the Argonauts, thus bridging the shadowy gap between myth and history. These places can still be identified today, particularly along the upper Bosphorus, where the strait and its shores show little evidence of modern civilization other than the argosies of oil-tankers and cargo-ships that pass through on their way to and from ports on the Black Sea, a commerce that began with the establishment of the first Greek colonies on the Euxine.

The first Greek colony on the Euxine was Sinope, today the Turkish city of Sinop, founded in the eighth century BC by Ionians from Miletos on the Aegean coast of Anatolia. During the following century Miletos founded some seventy colonies around the shores of the Euxine and the Propontis, while other Greek cities added a few more foundations there and also on the Hellespont and the Bosphorus. The first Greek colony on the Bosphorus was Chalcedon, founded by Megara c. 675 BC on the Asian side of the strait where it flows into the Propontis. This colony survives today as Kadıköy, an Asian suburb of Istanbul, long eclipsed by the ancient imperial capital across the strait, the city originally known as Byzantium.

The original site of Byzantium was on the acropolis above Sarayburnu, the First Hill of the ancient city. Cursory archaeological excavations on the First Hill have revealed that the acropolis was first inhabited in the late Mycenaean period, c. 1300 BC. This may have been a Mycenaean trading-station, for several of these entrepots have been discovered in recent years along the Aegean

THE BOSPHORUS AND THE CITY

coast of Anatolia. But the Mycenaean remains on the First Hill and at another site on the upper reaches of the Golden Horn have never been carefully studied, and so for the moment one might conclude that these were short-lived trading-stations such as those that the Mycenaeans established elsewhere on the western shores of Anatolia at the time. A mention by Pliny indicates that in the ninth century BC there was a settlement named Lygos under the First Hill on the Golden Horn, probably a fishing village that was absorbed by Byzantium after it was founded by Byzas, known as the Megarian.

According to tradition, Byzantium was founded by Byzas in 658 BC, seventeen years after the establishment of Chalcedon, when he led a second expedition from Megara to set up a colony on the Bosphorus. Before he set out on this venture Byzas went to Delphi to consult the oracle of Apollo, who advised him to settle "opposite the land of the blind." The oracle was referring to the people of Chalcedon, who must have been blind not to have seen the much greater advantages of the site on the European side of the strait, and so Byzas established the new Megarian colony on the acropolis hill at the confluence of the Bosphorus and the Golden Horn. One of the advantages offered by this site was its greater defensibility, for the steep acropolis there was protected by the sea on all sides except to the west, where a defense wall could be erected. Another advantage was that the Golden Horn provided a superb natural harbor, shielded from storms by the hilly land that enclosed it on all sides except where it opened onto the Bosphorus, and there the promontory below the acropolis curves around to the north to shield the inner port. This promontory also acts as a barrier to divert the shoals of tunny that swim down the Bosphorus from the Black Sea, forcing them into the port and creating an abundant fishery that became one of the principal sources of income for the people of Byzantium. Other important sources of income were the tolls and harbor fees paid by the ships that passed through the strait, for Byzantium controlled the Bosphorus from the very beginning of its history, and this was the principal reason

10   THE BOSPHORUS AND THE CITY

for its subsequent rise to greatness. As Gyllius pointed out: "The Bosphorus is the first creator of Byzantium, greater and more important than Byzas, the founder of the city."

The history of the Greek city of Byzantium lasted for nearly a thousand years. Then a new age in the history of the city began in the year AD 330, when Constantine the Great moved the capital of his empire from Rome to Byzantium. Thereafter Byzantium was called Constantinople, the City of Constantine, serving as capital of the realm that came to be known as the Byzantine Empire. Constantinople was capital of the Byzantine Empire through the next eleven centuries, except for the years 1204-61, when the city was occupied by the Venetians and the Latin knights of the Fourth Crusade. The Byzantine Empire came to an end in 1453, when Constantinople was captured by the Ottoman Turks under Sultan Mehmet II, known to the Turks as Fatih, or the Conqueror. After the Conquest Fatih rebuilt and repopulated the city, now known as Istanbul, which thus became capital of the Ottoman Empire. Istanbul remained the capital until the Ottoman Empire ended in 1923, to be replaced by the new Republic of Turkey founded by Kemal Atatürk and his followers. The capital of the Republic was then established in Ankara, but Istanbul continued as the principal city of Turkey, with the monuments of two vanished empires on its skyline to remind travellers of its former greatness. As Gyllius wrote as an encomium to the ancient imperial capital on the Bosphorus: "'It seems to me that while other cities are mortal, this one will remain as long as there are men on earth."

CHAPTER TWO
THE GALATA BRIDGE TO KABATAŞ

Most travelers setting out to explore the Bosphorus (in Turkish, Boğaziçi) for the first time take a ferry from the main *iskele*, or landing, on the Stamboul shore of the Golden Horn below the Galata Bridge. Depending on the time of day, these ferries stop at a number of *iskele*s on both the European and Asian shores of the Bosphorus on their way up and down the strait. En route one sees virtually all of the monuments along the Bosphorus, but only for a few fleeting moments, and to examine them in more detail one must travel along the shore roads on later trips. And then to see the upper Bosphorus, which is inaccessible by either road or ferry, one must hire a boat at one of the villages at the last *iskele*s, a true voyage of exploration, for there are few evidences of modern civilization on the upper strait, where many of the landmarks have associations with the journey of Jason and the Argonauts, and there Gyllius is the best guide. And so in the chapters that follow the description will combine the points of view of travelers seeing the strait either from the sea or along the shore roads, as far as they go, beginning at the Galata Bridge.

The area from which the ferries leave was in early Byzantine times known as Neorion, the principal harbor of Constantinople. Farther along towards Sarayburnu was Klistos Limin, the Enclosed Port, which was filled in during the third quarter of the nineteenth century to create the freight yard for the railway line. This was also known as the Prosphorean Haven, the original port of the ancient town of Byzantium. The only monument that has survived along this shore is the seaside pavilion at the far end of the freight yard. This is Sepetçiler Kasrı, the Kiosk of the Basket-Weavers, now the International Press Center. This was built in 1643 for Sultan Ibrahim the Mad (1640-48) by the

12   THE GALATA BRIDGE TO KABATAŞ

Eminönü: *İskele*s with Topkapı Sarayı in the
background and the Sepetçiler Kasrı (left)

The Haghia Sophia (left) and Topkapı Sarayı (center)

Guild of Basket-Weavers. The vaulted chambers beneath the pavilion house the *pazar kayık*s, the imperial barges that were used to row the Sultan to his seaside palaces along the Bosphorus and the Golden Horn. The rear wall of the pavilion has Greek inscriptions dating from the ninth century AD, indicating that it was originally part of the Byzantine defense wall along the Golden Horn, which at Sarayburnu linked up with the fortifications along the Marmara. Sepetçiler Kasrı was one of the sea pavilions of Topkapı Sarayı, whose walled courtyards and kiosks we see among the groves of cypresses on the summit of the First Hill, the acropolis of ancient Byzantium.

As the ferry starts out across the harbor toward the Bosphorus we have a rapidly changing view of the port and its surroundings. Behind at the Stamboul end of the Galata Bridge is Yeni Cami, the New Mosque, built for the Valide Sultan (Queen Mother) Turhan Hatice, mother of Mehmet IV (1648-87), and completed in 1663. The mosque is the principal landmark in Eminönü, the old market quarter around the Stamboul end of the Galata Bridge. During the latter centuries of the Byzantine era this area was given over to several Italian city states for their concessions, which comprised residences, warehouses and docks along the Golden Horn. The area by the present *iskele* was the concession of the Genoese, who also controlled the town of Galata on the opposite shore of the Golden Horn. The area just below the bridge was the concession of the Pisans. Beyond that was a small strip controlled by the Amalfians, and above the bridge a much larger quarter belonging to the Venetians. Wedged in between the concessions of the Amalfians and the Venetians was a narrow strip reserved for the Karaite Jews, who broke off from the main body of orthodox Jewry in the medieval Byzantine era. The Karaite Jews were displaced in the first half of the seventeenth century when construction began on Yeni Cami; they were then moved some distance up the Golden Horn on the north bank, in the village of Hasköy, where their descendants still live.

On the other side of the Golden Horn the skyline is domi-

14 THE GALATA BRIDGE TO KABATAŞ

The Port of Constantinople

Mosque of Sultan Valide, from the Port

THE GALATA BRIDGE TO KABATAŞ 15

nated by the conical-capped Galata Tower, which rises above the hill that dominates the entrance to the Golden Horn from the Bosphorus. The tower was built in 1340 by the Genoese, who in the latter centuries of the Byzantine era created an independent city-state in Galata, ruled by a Podesta, an official sent out annually from the mother city of Genoa. The tower was the focal point of a series of defense walls that extended from it to the Golden Horn on one side and the Bosphorus on the other, with additional fortifications added successively along the shore and between the main walls, thus creating six enceintes. The sixth and last of these enceintes, created in 1446, just seven years before the Turkish Conquest, extended from the present Galata Bridge to what is now Tophane, which still marks the northern limit of Galata along the shore of the Bosphorus.

During the Byzantine era the mouth of the Golden Horn was during times of siege closed by a great chain that extended from Sarayburnu to the Castle of Galata, a fortress at the confluence of the Horn and the Bosphorus in what is now Karaköy, the area around the Galata end of the bridge. It is believed that the site of the castle is that of Yeraltı Camii, the Underground Mosque; this is about 200 meters from the Galata Bridge, approached by walking along Rıhtım Caddesi past the *iskele* of the Denizcilik Bankası (Turkish Maritime Lines), and then turning left to cross Kemankeş Caddesi, where we see its entrance on the left.

The mosque is housed in the subterranean keep of a Byzantine structure, which some scholars have identified as the Castle of Galata, constructed by the Emperor Tiberius II (578-82). Descending into the mosque, we find ourselves in a maze of dark narrow passageways between a forest of squat columns supporting low vaults, six rows of nine each, or 54 in all. Toward the rear of the mosque there are two large chambers separated from the rest of the interior by grills. These are the tombs of two sainted Muslim martyrs, Abu Sufyan and Amiri Wahibi, both of whom are supposed to have died in the first Arab siege of Constantinople in 674-78. The site of their graves was revealed

16   THE GALATA BRIDGE TO KABATAŞ

The Tower of Galata

Galata: The Galata Tower with the Customs House in the foreground

in a dream to a Nakşibendi dervish one night in 1640. When Murat IV (1623-40) learned of this he had the graves opened and the saints reinterred in a shrine on the site; then in 1757 the whole dungeon was converted into a mosque by the Grand Vezir Köse Mustafa Paşa.

Walking away from the Bosphorus to the main thoroughfare, Kemeraltı Caddesi, on the far side of the avenue we see a church with a tall tower. This is the church of St. Benoit, founded by the Benedictines in 1427; later it became the royal chapel of the French ambassadors to the Ottoman Empire, several of whom are buried there. After being in the hands of the Jesuits for several centuries, it was given, on the temporary suppression of that order in 1773, to the Lazarists, to whom it still belongs. In 1804 they established a school next to the church; this is still in operation and continues to be one of the best foreign lycees in the city. Only the tower remains from the original fifteenth-century building, with the rest of the church dating from two later reconstructions: the nave and south aisle in 1732, and the north aisle in 1871.

Turning right on Kemeraltı Caddesi, we see on the right a fine modern church built of gleaming white stone. This is the Armenian church of Surp Kirkor Lusavoriç, St. Gregory the Illuminator, erected in 1960 after the original church had been demolished to widen the avenue. The new building is a replica of the famous church of St. Gregory at Etchmiadzin in Armenia, a seventh-century edifice that is one of the masterpieces of medieval Armenian architecture.

The quarter between Kemeraltı Caddesi and the Bosphorus is a labyrinth of narrow winding streets in which it is impossible to give specific directions. By wandering through the neighborhood behind St. Gregory we come upon three Greek churches of some interest. These are the churches of St. John the Baptist, St. Nicholas, and the Panayia (the Blessed Virgin), all three of which were founded in the fifteenth or sixteenth centuries, although the present structures date from the nineteenth century. The most in-

18 THE GALATA BRIDGE TO KABATAŞ

teresting of these is the church of the Panayia, which is enclosed within a high courtyard wall. Notice over the main gate to the courtyard the curious symbol beside the name of the church: a cross with the star and crescent in the upper right-hand corner. This is the symbol of the Turkish Orthodox Church; this sect was founded in 1922 by a dissident Anatolian priest known as Papa Eftim, who took his parishioners with him in a schism with the Greek Orthodox Church. During the half-century from that time until his death, Papa Eftim, who styled himself Patriarch Efthemios I, engaged in a running battle with the Ecumenical Patriarchate, in the course of which he won control of the neighboring churches of St. John and St. Nicholas. The Turkish Orthodox Church has now dwindled to just a small number, mostly old people who were part of Papa Eftim's original supporters, all of whom were Karamanlı, Turkish-speaking Christians from Anatolia. The mass that is celebrated in the three churches is in Turkish rather than Greek, though the liturgy is exactly the same as in the Greek Orthodox Church. The most treasured possession of the church of the Panayia is an icon of the Virgin Hodeghetria, the Guide or Teacher, known as the Black Virgin because it is blackened with age; this is believed to have been brought from Kaffa in the Crimea by the original Greek congregation who founded the church here in Galata in the late fifteenth century.

Continuing along Kemeraltı Caddesi and crossing to the left side, we soon come to Hendek Sokağı, the Street of the Moat. The name stems from the fact that the street follows the course of the moat that once extended around the walls of Genoese Galata. A fragment of the medieval fortifications still survives in the structure of the coffeehouse at the street corner. This was part of a tower that formed the junction between the walls extending along the Bosphorus and those coming down from the Galata Tower on the hill above.

At this point we have reached the outer bounds of what was once the quarter of medieval Galata along the shore of the Bosphorus. Those who are travelling by ferry along this stretch

THE GALATA BRIDGE TO KABATAŞ 19

will have passed the Yolcu Salonu, the main passenger terminal of the Turkish Maritime Lines, and beyond that the docks of the lower Bosphorus. This stretch of the Bosphorus was paralleled by the sea walls of the sixth enceinte of the walled Genoese town of Galata, which ended where Tophane İskelesi Caddesi turns in from Kemankeş Caddesi. This brings us to Tophane, the first locality along the European shore of the Bosphorus beyond Galata.

The principal monument in Tophane is the *külliye*, or mosque complex, of Kılıç Ali Paşa, which is to the southwest of the intersection of Tophane İskele Caddesi and Necatibey Caddesi. The *külliye* was built in 1580-81 by the great Ottoman architect Sinan, who was then at least eighty-three years old. (Various scholars put Sinan's birthdate as early as 1490 and as late as 1497, the latter now being the generally accepted date.). The founder was Kılıç (the Sword) Ali Paşa, one of the great admirals in Ottoman history. Born in Calabria in 1497 of Christian parents, he was captured in his youth by Algerian pirates and spent fourteen years as a galley slave. After regaining his freedom he joined Süleyman's service as a buccaneer, becoming a Muslim and changing his name to Uluç Ali. He distinguished himself in several naval engagements, and as a reward he was made an admiral and was also given the post of Governor of Algiers. He was the only Turkish commander to distinguish himself at the disastrous Ottoman defeat by the allied Christian fleet at the battle of Lepanto in 1571. As a result of this Selim II (1566-74) appointed him Kaptan Paşa, the commanding admiral of the Ottoman navy, and renamed him Kılıç Ali because at Lepanto he had cut through the Christian fleet like a veritable sword.

While serving as Governor of Algiers Ali Paşa came into contact with Miguel Cervantes, who had been enslaved there after his capture at the battle of Lepanto. Five years after being brought to Algiers Cervantes managed to escape, but he was recaptured and brought before Ali Paşa. Ali Paşa took pity on Cervantes, releasing him from captivity and giving him enough money to make his way home. Cervantes paid tribute to the kindness of

20 THE GALATA BRIDGE TO KABATAŞ

Ali Paşa in Chapter 32 of *Don Quixote*, where "The captive relates his life and adventures."

The climax of Ali Paşa's career came in 1573, when he recaptured Tunis from Don Juan of Austria. Seven years later he retired to Istanbul, at which point he decided to build his mosque complex. When Ali Paşa asked permission from Murat III (1574-95) to build his mosque, so the story goes, the Sultan sarcastically suggested that he construct it on the sea since that was the Kaptan Paşa's domain. Ali Paşa proceeded to do just that, and commissioned Sinan to build him a mosque complex on land that he had filled in along the shore of the Bosphorus in Tophane. The complex originally was situated right on the seaside, but because of further filling-in operations in the past century it is now some distance in from the shore.

The *külliye* consists of a mosque, a *türbe* (tomb), a *medrese* (theological school), and a *hamam* (public bath). The precinct wall encloses the mosque and the *türbe* behind it; the *hamam* is across the street to the southwest, with the *medrese* to its rear.

The mosque is preceded by a very picturesque double porch. The outer porch has a deeply sloping penthouse roof, supported by twelve columns on the front and three on each side, all with lozenge capitals; in its center is a monumental marble portal, and there are bronze grills between the columns. The inner porch is of the usual type, with five domed bays supported by columns capped with stalactite capitals. Above the entrance portal is the historical inscription giving the date of foundation of the mosque, and above this is a text from the Koran in a fascinating calligraphy, set in a curious projecting frame, triangular in shape and adorned with stalactites.

On entering the mosque we find ourselves in a pseudo-narthex of five cross-vaulted bays, separated from the main prayer area by four rectangular piers. The central area is covered by the dome, 12.7 meters in diameter, supported by four huge piers, with pendentives making the transition to the circular cornice. Semi-domes open out from the great circular arches at either end, with a conch covering the little rectangular apse at the far end, which encloses the *mihrap*, the niche that indicates *kıble*, the direction of Mecca. On either side of the central area pairs of columns between the pillars support an ogive-arched arcade, which extends around the rear of the room between the four piers of the pseudonarthex. Above this is the gallery, which at the sides has twice as many arched openings as the side aisles below, both levels having six bays. At the rear right-hand corner of the prayer area is the gallery of the *müezzin*s, or chanters, carried on eight delicate columns of white marble. To the right of the *mihrap*, as is customary, is the conical-capped *mimber*, or pulpit, approached by a flight of steps from which the imam at the time of the Friday noon prayer gives the *hutbe*, or weekly sermon.

The *hamam* of the *külliye* still functions as a public bath, having been in continuous operation now for more than four centuries. Evliya Çelebi (1611- c. 1680), the incomparable Turkish chronicler, writes of the *hamam* in his *Seyahatname*, or *Narrative of Travels:* "The bath of Ali Paşa is a clean well-served bath frequented by all classes." Its plan is unique among all of Sinan's extant *hamam*s. Ordinarily a *hamam* has three distinct sections, which are usually laid out one after the other on a straight line. The first is the *camekân*, which is used as a reception and dressing room, and where one recovers and relaxes after the bath. Next comes the *soğukluk*, a chamber of intermediate temperature, which serves as an anteroom to the bath, keeping the cold air out on one side and the hot air in on the other. Finally there is the *hararet*, or steam room, where the bathers sweat it out lying on a stone platform called the *göbektaşı*, or belly stone, which is heated from the furnace below. The *camekân* is usually the most monumental chamber, typically a large square room covered by a dome; the *soğukluk* is almost always a mere passageway; while the *hararet* is invariably the most elaborate room, often cruciform in plan. The layout of the three rooms is most unusual in Ali Paşa's *hamam*. From the vast domed *camekân,* doors lead into two separate *soğukluk*s, lying not between the two end chambers as is customary, but on either side of the *hararet*, each of them consisting of three domed rooms of different sizes. The *hararet*, instead of having the usual cruciform plan, is hexagonal with open bathing places in four of its six arched recesses, the other giving access from the two *soğukluk*s.

The *medrese*, which now serves as a clinic, appears to be a later addition to the *külliye*, built in the early seventeenth century and thus not a work of Sinan, who died in 1588. It is square in plan, with the students' cells (*hücre*) opening off an arcaded courtyard with a fountain at the center. The large domed chamber at the east side of the square is the *dershane*, or lecture room.

The *türbe* is a plain but elegant domed building of octagonal plan, with alternately one and two windows in each facade, in two tiers. In the main burial chamber, which is preceded by a porch, there are two cenotaphs, the largest one in the center covering the grave of Kılıç Ali Paşa. Ali Paşa was buried here in 1587, after having died in a moment of passion, according to the historian Josef von Hammer: "Although ninety years of age, he had not been able to renounce the pleasures of the *harem*, and he died in the arms of a concubine." Evliya Çelebi gives a colorful description of the old buccaneer in his latter years, in a section of the *Seyahatname* entitled "In praise of Ali Paşa:"

He was a most simple and believing man, whose original name of Uluç was changed to Kılıç. At the first Friday prayer of his newly-finished mosque, when the singer of the *Na'at*, or antiphon in the Prophet's praise, began in the highest tone, Ali Paşa stood up, and directing himself to the singer, asked, 'What is all that bawling for, are we in a tavern or an ale-house?' The Vezirs near him said, 'My lord, he sings the praises of the Prophet.' 'Well,' said he, 'is Mister Mohammed pleased with this bawling?' and as they answered, 'Yes,' he asked 'How much have I written down for his pay? Look into the register.' They replied, 'Ten paras.' 'Well,' said he, 'how much have I assigned to that fellow who praises our Emperor Murat?' They said, 'Forty aspers.' 'Well, which is greater, the Lord Emperor or Mister Mohammed?' Having been answered, 'that the Prophet was yet greater than the Emperor,' he said, 'Well then put the Imperial and Prophetical brawlers on the same footing of forty aspers.' This jest is known among the wits. Every Friday he used to sit on the exterior *sofa* of his mosque and distribute a purse among the poor.

Directly across the avenue from Kılıç Ali Paşa Camii is a little mosque known as Karabaş Mescidi. The mosque was founded in 1530 by Karabaş Mustafa Ağa, who was Chief Black Eunuch in the reign of Süleyman the Magnificent. It is rectangular in plan with a hipped roof. The mosque was restored in 1962.

Across the street north of Kılıç Ali Paşa Camii is one of the most famous of the baroque street fountains of Istanbul, known as Tophane Çeşmesi. Built in 1732 by Mahmut I (1730-54), it has marble walls completely covered with floral designs and arabesques carved in low relief and originally painted and gilded. Its charmingly domed and widely overhanging roof was lacking for many years but has recently been restored. The fountain with the mosque behind and the busy and picturesque throngs around the port used to be a favorite subject with etchers in the nineteenth century.

On the heights above the other side of Necatibey Caddesi we see the multi-domed structure from which the surrounding quarter takes its name; this is Tophane, the Cannon-House, once the principal military foundry in the Ottoman Empire. The original foundry on this site was built by Mehmet II (1451-81) soon after the Conquest. It was extended and improved by Beyazit II (1481-1512), but was then demolished by Süleyman the Magnificent (1520-66), who replaced it with a larger and more modern establishment in preparation for his campaigns of conquest. As Evliya writes in his *Seyahatname:*

In the time of Süleyman I, who governed forty-six years, all kings and monarchs yielded peacefully to his power, with the exception of the

24 THE GALATA BRIDGE TO KABATAŞ

Emperor of Germany, who continued at war with him. Of these forty-six years, Süleyman had passed four in making war in Arabia, four in Persia, four against the Venetians, and thirty-four against the Emperor of Germany. These Germans are strong, warlike, cunning, devilish, coarse infidels, who, excelling in artillery, Sultan Süleyman endeavored to equal by assembling gunners and artillerymen by rich presents from all countries. He pulled down the gun-foundry built by his ancestors, Mehmet II and Beyazit II, and built a new one which no one, who has not seen it, is able to judge of what may be accomplished by human strength and understanding. It is situated on a height, one hundred paces from the shore, surrounded by walls so strong that it could resist any siege. In the middle of it rises a square building forty cubits high, covered by a roof in the shape of an ass's back, through which large furnace chimneys give escape to the smoke of the work shops. On the roof, upon which you can walk, are many hundred casks of water in case of fire, occasioned by sparks from the chimneys, and which could be immediately extinguished by the people who keep watch over it.

Evliya then goes on to give a fascinating account of the techniques and rituals involved in the casting of the largest siege-cannon:

On both sides of the furnaces with the cupolas are placed immense piles of wood, cut a year before and well dried. On the day of founding, all the masters, journeymen, the General of the Artillery, the first guardian, the imam, *müezzin*, and time-keeper assemble, and while they cry 'Allah! Allah!' the wood is thrown into the ovens. After being heated by burning for twenty-four hours, the founders and fire workers strip naked, put on their slippers only, and an odd kind of cap which leaves only the eyes visible, and a thick kind of sleeves; because the fire having raged in the furnaces twenty-four hours, no person is enabled to approach them on account of the heat, if not dressed in like manner. Whoever wishes to see a fine specimen of the infernal fire, must look at this. The twenty-four hours having elapsed, notice is given to the vezirs, the mufti, and sheikhs; forty persons and the founders are admitted within, and the rest of the servants are shut out, because the metal when in fusion does not bear to be looked on with evil eyes....

The masters then desire the vezirs and sheikhs, who sit on sofas at a great distance, to repeat continually the words: 'There is no power and no strength but in God.' The masters then with wooden shovels throw some hundred quintals of tin into the sea of molten brass, and the head founder says to the Grand Vezir, the other vezirs, and sheikhs, 'Throw as alms for the true faith some of your gold and silver coins into the brazen sea.' The Grand Vezir then gives him some purses of gold, as does the Head Treasurer from the Emperor's side, and each of the other vezirs gives one or two purses of gold and silver to the head founder, who throws them in, before their eyes, into the molten brass, saying, 'In God's name.' Poles like the yard-arms of ships are used for mingling the gold and silver with the base metal, and are replaced as fast as they are consumed. As soon as the surface of the brass begins to bubble, the masters know that it is in a complete state of fusion, more wood is thrown into the fire as before, great care being taken that not a drop of water is to be found among it, because a drop of water thrown into the molten brass would burst all the forms, and destroy all those who are present. On both sides of the oven forty to fifty sheep are kept ready. All the vezirs, sheikhs and the rest of the company rise. The timekeeper gives notice to the master of the furnace half an hour before it is time to open the mouth of it; the Imam repeats the accustomed prayers and all the assembled cry, 'Amen!' All are very fervent and zealous in their prayers, because it is a most dangerous business, in which many masters and vezirs have perished. The time fixed having expired and been announced by the time keeper, the head founder and masters, dressed in their clumsy dresses of keche, open the mouth of the furnace with iron hooks, saying 'Allah, Allah!' The metal beginning to flow, covers the faces of the men with a glare at a hundred paces distance. The vezirs and sheikhs take white sheets and sacrifice the sheep on both sides of the oven. The metal flows from canal to canal into the form, which if the largest is filled in half an hour; the flowing brass is then stopped by an oily mass of clay and flows to the next form. Prayers are said again, and so till the end, when seventy robes of honor are distributed

26 THE GALATA BRIDGE TO KABATAŞ

and augmentations of pay are decreed; their dresses of keche are taken off and the General of Artillery gives a feast for the Grand Vezir. The cannon remain a week in the mould, after which they are taken out and polished. The joiners then take the cannon into their care like beloved children, and make them ready for war.

Süleyman's foundry has long since disappeared; the present structure was built by Selim III (1789-1807) in 1803, part of his program to modernize and reform the Ottoman army. The foundry is a large rectangular building of brick and stone, covered by eight great domes supported by three lofty piers. The building was partly restored some years ago, and there are plans to reopen it as part of the Military Museum in ·Harbiye, but at the moment it remains closed.

Beyond the foundry itself, along the heights overlooking the avenue, we see a series of ruined substructures, walls and domes; these once formed part of the general complex of the Tophane military base, which included extensive barracks for the artillerymen. Evliya also describes the barracks of the artillerymen at Tophane, as well as some of the cannon that are still displayed there on the heights above the avenue.

The barracks of the artillerymen were, like the foundry, built by Mehmet II, Beyazit II and Süleyman I.... Inside are rooms inhabited by colonels, captains, veterans, cooks and artillerymen; they dress like the Janissaries, in leather gowns, and wear knives with silver chains. They are the bravest troops, and in twenty-two battles, wherein I was present, I saw no braver, because, when the enemy, pointing their guns on ours, swept away forty or fifty gunners at a discharge, they were as busy at their guns as ants. Sultan İbrahim, on a visit to the foundry, having taken his lodgings in the kiosk above the gateway, this kiosk has been reserved for the Emperor. At the time when Hafız Ahmet Paşa went against Baghdad, there were no less than seventeen hundred guns, every one worth the tribute of a province, beside sixty so large that cobblers and other poor men make their lodgings in them. These guns are shaded by

THE GALATA BRIDGE TO KABATAŞ 27

planes and cypress trees, by linden trees and willows. On the second day of the Bayram many thousand persons assemble here, and stretch themselves on the ground of the walk. The artillery is one of the greatest treasures of the Ottoman Empire.

Across the avenue there is a small kiosk in the Empire style, originally part of the Tophane complex. This was built by Sultan Abdülaziz (1861-76) as a review pavilion, from which he could watch parades of the artillerymen from the barracks of the Tophane arsenal across the avenue.

Beyond the kiosk is Nusretiye Camii, the Mosque of Victory. This was built between 1822 and 1826 for Mahmut II (1808-39); it was completed just after the Sultan's extermination of the Janissaries, the rebellious elite corps of the old Ottoman army, and its name commemorates that event. The mosque was designed and erected by Kirkor Balyan, the founder of the large family of Armenian architects who served the sultans through most of the nineteenth century, building most of the late Ottoman imperial mosques and palaces one sees today along the shores of the Bosphorus. Kirkor Balyan had studied in Paris and his mosque shows a curious blend of baroque and Empire motifs, highly unTurkish, but not without charm. In building Nusretiye Camii he abandoned the traditional arrangement of a monumental courtyard and substituted an elaborate series of palace-like apartments in two stories; these form the front facade of the building, a feature that became a characteristic of all the Balyan mosques. Among the noteworthy features are the bulbous weight-towers, the jutting dome arches, the overly slender minarets (they were so slender that they fell down soon after construction and had to be reerected), the ornate bronze grills, and in the interior the abundance of marble garlands in the Empire style, along with the *mimber*, a marvelous baroque creation.

Tophane, like all of the other former villages on the European shore of the lower Bosphorus, has now been amalgamated into the urban mass of Istanbul. But we can evoke something of the character of these places in Ottoman times by reading Evliya Çelebi's *Seyahatname*, as in his description of Tophane and Fındıklı, the next village up the Bosphorus:

At Tophane and Fındıklı there are in all eight hundred shops but no *bedesten*. The fruit shops are famous for their elegance, and are shaded by large trees. Among the exquisite niceties of this place are its roast meat, sherbet, buza and white bread, light as sponge. The famous baker of this white bread, İsa Çelebi, received a boon from a dervish, by the power of which everything he undertook was a success; he became the baker of the world, because his bread is carried to Isfahan, and though the journey takes three months it does not spoil.

The greatest number of the inhabitants of Tophane are merchants, sailors and merchantmen, flocking together from the shores of the Black Sea... and a great number of Georgians and Abaza. The Abaza, to keep their children from growing up like the boys of Constantinople, send every year those of one or two years with their nurses on board ship to their own country, to be brought up there until they are fifteen years old, when they are brought back to Constantinople and sold, or offered as presents to the great men and favorites of the Emperor. Lo! Our late Melek Ahmet Paşa [Grand Vezir of Murat IV] and Siyavuş Paşa were Abaza, born at Tophane and brought up in their own country. In proportion to the size of Tophane it has but few fountains and marketplaces, but the houses are all provided with wells. The best houses are those of Cihangir and Ayas Paşa; they rise one behind the other and are surrounded by gardens. The streets are all paved like those at Constantinople; the roads are wide, and the mosques are near to one another, for the people are pious. The great men wear splendid costumes, and the merchants dress according to their revenue. The women wear the cloak, *ferajah,* with a turban on the head and a veil before their faces, and thus are very well dressed; they are also very amiable.

Some 400 meters farther along Necatibey Caddesi we see on the height above the avenue Cihangir Camii, which has given its name to the surrounding quarter. The original mosque on this site was built by Sinan in 1553 for Süleyman the Magnificent, who dedicated it to the memory of his son Prince Cihangir. Cihangir had died earlier that year out of sorrow, it was said, for his beloved half-brother, the unfortunate Prince Mustafa, whom Süleyman had executed on suspicion of trying to usurp the throne. The original mosque was rebuilt after fires in 1720 and several times thereafter in the eighteenth and nineteenth centuries. The present rather exceptionally ugly mosque was built in 1890 by Abdülhamit II (1876-1909); in the dedicatory inscription over the entrance portal the Sultan boasts that his new edifice is "bigger and better than the old ones" that it replaced.

Evliya tells an apocryphal story about a Christian convent that he says stood on the heights where Tophane and Cihangir Camii were later built, and in so doing he gives us his bizarre theory as to how the Bosphorus was first formed.

Tophane in the time of the infidels was a convent situated in the middle of a forest; this was called Cihang; as it was dedicated to St. Alexander the infidels visit it once a year on the feast of this saint. A tradition says that Alexander the Great enchained at this spot magicians and witches from Gog and Magog by throwing mountains on them with the incumbence to take to the sea during the forty days of deepest winter in order to watch the seas surrounding Constantinople; but these demons, having cut the mountains which shut up the Black Sea, it broke in by the Bosphorus.... Thus the foundation of Tophane is carried back to Alexander.

Evliya then goes on to describe the original mosque of Cihangir, throwing in an interesting tale of adventure in the bargain.

The mosque of Cihangir, which is on the spot of Alexander's Convent, was built by Sultan Süleyman, who dedicated it to the memory of his son Cihangir; it stands on a high hill, which is ascended by a flight of one hundred steps from the mosque of Mehmet Ağa, situated on the seashore. On some places along the steps there are seats for reposing, because it is extremely difficult to ascend this height without rest. Notwithstanding the steepness and narrowness of the way, a strange fellow once rode up to it, who, having killed someone in the marketplace of Salihpazar, was pursued to this place, where his pursuers stopped because they believed it was impossible to get up the height on horseback. Nevertheless he rode up it in a miraculous manner, and made his escape. The square mosque is covered with a light cupola and has a fine minaret. The courtyard is adorned with plane trees. In the afternoon people assemble here to look at the ships on the sea; it is the work of the architect Sinan.

Some 300 meters beyond Cihangir Camii we come to Fındıklı, another former seaside village that has been amalgamated into the urban mass of Istanbul. Fındıklı was known in Byzantine times as Argyropolis, the City of Silver. This name was given to it by the Patriarch Atticus (406-25), because it stood directly across the Bosphorus from Chrysopolis, the City of Gold, today's Üsküdar, the great Anatolian suburb of Istanbul. According to Greek tradition, this is where St. Andrew the Apostle landed when he came to Byzantium, and it was here that he appointed St. Stachys as the first bishop of the city.

On the right side of Necatibey Caddesi here is Mimar Sinan University, named in honor of the great Ottoman architect (in Turkish, *mimar*). The university houses the Güzel Sanatlar Akademisi, or Fine Arts Academy, which has an exhibition hall opening out onto the Bosphorus where art exhibitions are held periodically.

A short way farther along on the right side of the avenue we see Molla Çelebi Camii. This elegant mosque was built by Sinan in 1565-66 for Molla Mehmet Efendi, Chief Justice in the reign of Süleyman the Magnificent. The *külliye* originally included a *hamam* and a *mektep*, or primary school, but both of these have vanished. The mosque is preceded by the customary porch of five domed bays. The building is hexagonal in plan, covered by a

THE GALATA BRIDGE TO KABATAŞ

Cihangir: Cihangir Camii

Fındıklı: Molla Çelebi Camii

dome supported by a pair of free-standing octagonal pillars at the rear, two engaged piers at the sides, and the inner corners of the projecting rectangular apse that contains the *mihrap*. The central dome is surrounded by five semidomes, two on either side between the pillars and one over the apsidal niche, the first four being of equal size and the fifth deeper.

A short distance beyond Molla Çelebi Camii, between the highway and the Bosphorus shore, we see another of Istanbul's baroque street-fountains, the Hekimoğlu Ali Paşa Çeşmesi. This was built in 1732 for Hekimoğlu Ali Paşa, Grand Vezir in the reign of Mahmut I. This is a beautifully carved work in white marble, with a *çeşme*, or wall-fountain, on two of its faces; unfortunately it has lost its quaint overhanging roof.

Directly across the highway there is a beautiful baroque *sebil*, or fountain-house. This was built in 1787 for Koca Yusuf Paşa, Grand Vezir in the reign of Abdülhamit I (1774-89). It has a magnificent *çeşme* in the center, flanked by the two grilled windows of the *sebil*, where attendants handed out cups of water free to passersby. The whole of the *sebil* is elaborately carved and decorated with encrustations of various marbles, with a long calligraphic inscription forming a frieze above the windows. Here, as elsewhere, the donor is identified as well as the poet who composed the inscription, which ends with an elaborate chronogram in which the numerical value of the Arabic letters gives the date of construction. After a recent restoration the *sebil* is now the center of a little outdoor café, pleasantly embowered in trees.

A short distance farther along we come to the Kabataş İskelesi, where ferries and water taxis cross the Bosphorus to Üsküdar. The name Kabataş comes from that of the sacred meteoric stone (*taş*) at the shrine of Kaaba in Mecca, though how it came to be associated with this place is unknown. In antiquity it was the port of Argyropolis and was known as Ajantion, after the hero Ajax (in Greek, Aias) of Salamis, son of Telamon. Ajax fought in the army of Agamemnon at Troy, where he went mad and committed suicide. He was worshipped as a semi-divine hero

THE GALATA BRIDGE TO KABATAŞ   33

by the Megarians, who erected an altar to him here when they founded Chalcedon. His father Telamon, King of Salamis, had been one of the heroes who accompanied Jason on his voyage on Argos. Another myth associated with this place concerns Chalkis, the inventor of the Byzantine zither, who charmed the dolphins of the Bosphorus with his music, and when one of them was killed by the shepherd Charandas he raised a memorial to it near Ajantion. These are all but forgotten myths, but one might recall the latter legend when seeing dolphins gamboling in the waves as they occasionally make their way up and down the Bosphorus.

Dolmabahçe: Dolmabahçe Camii

CHAPTER THREE
KABATAŞ TO BEBEK

Some 200 meters beyond the Kabataş pier along the shore we come to Dolmabahçe Camii. This was built in 1853 for the Bezmiâlem Valide Sultan, mother of Sultan Abdülmecit (1839-61); the architect was Nikogos Balyan, grandson of Kirkor Balyan, builder of Nusretiye Camii. Nikogos Balyan came at an unfortunate period in the development of late Ottoman architecture, and it is only with difficulty that one can admire any of his buildings. The great cartwheel arches of the mosque seem particularly disagreeable; but the two very slender Corinthian minarets, one at each end of the little palace-like structure that precedes the mosque, have a certain charm.

Directly across the avenue from Dolmabahçe Camii there is a tiny *külliye* with a *sebil* as its dominant structure. This was built in 1741 by the Sipahi (cavalry knight) Hacı Mehmet Emin Ağa. The Turkish architectural historian Halil Ethem says rightly that this is "perhaps the most interesting eighteenth-century *sebil* in Istanbul." The five-windowed *sebil* is flanked symmetrically by a door on one side and by a *çeşme* on the other; there follow three grilled windows opening into a small graveyard for the members of the Sipahi's family, his own tomb being, most unusually, in the *sebil* itself. Beyond the graveyard there was once a small *mektep*, now vanished. The whole of the *sebil* is handsomely carved and decorated with various marbles; it was restored in the mid-1970s and is now the center of a very pleasant outdoor café.

The baroque clock-tower along the shore north of Dolmabahçe Camii was also erected by Nikogos Balyan; completed in 1854, it is made of cut stone and has a height of 27 meters, making it one of the most prominent landmarks on the European shore of the Bosphorus.

We now come to Dolmabahçe Sarayı, the largest and grandest

KABATAŞ TO BEBEK

by far of all the imperial Ottoman palaces on the Bosphorus. The main entrance to the palace is through the gardens, just beyond the clock tower.

The present site of the palace and its grounds was originally a small harbor on the Bosphorus. On 22 April 1453, during the Ottoman siege of Constantinople, Mehmet II had seventy ships of his fleet anchored here in preparation for the stratagem that turned the tide of battle in his favor. After sunset that day he had the ships placed on wheeled platforms and hauled by oxen, pulling them over the heights of Galata and then down to the Golden Horn, thus bypassing the chain that the Byzantines had stretched from the promontory below the acropolis to the Castle of Galata. This gave the Turks control of the Golden Horn, setting the stage for their final conquest of Constantinople on 29 May of that year. After Fatih's time the area became a royal garden. Evliya says that Selim I (1512-20) built a kiosk here, and Gyllius mentions that in his time it was known as the Little Valley of the Royal Garden. It was Ahmet I (1603-17) who began to fill in the small harbor in order to extend his gardens, and the filling-in process was continued by his son, Osman II (1618-22). As Evliya writes, explaining the origin of the name Dolmabahçe, which means "filled-in garden:"

By order of Sultan Osman II all ships of the fleet, and all merchant ships at the time in the harbor of Constantinople, were obliged to load with stones, which were thrown into the sea before Dolmabahçe, so that a space of 400 yards was filled up with stones where the sea formed a bay, and the place was called 'the filled-in garden', or Dolmabahçe.

Evliya goes on to tell one of his astonishing stories about Murat IV, his unpredictable patron: "Sultan Murat IV happened once to be reading at Dolmabahçe the satirical work *Sohami* of Nefii Efendi when lightning struck the ground near him; being terrified he threw the book in the sea and then gave orders to Bayram Paşa to strangle the author Nefii Efendi."

By the beginning of the nineteenth century there was a large

Dolma-Batche, from the Necropolis of Pera

Dolmabahçe: Dolmabahçe Sarayı

imperial summer residence at Dolmabahçe, and Mahmut II seems to have preferred this to the old palace of Topkapı Sarayı. His son and successor Abdülmecit decided to move out of Topkapı Sarayı altogether, and in 1842 he commissioned Karabet Balyan (son of Kirkor Balyan) and his son Nikogos to replace the existing structures at Dolmabahçe with a new palace. The new palace of Dolmabahçe was completed in 1853, whereupon the Sultan and his household moved in there, abandoning the old Saray on the First Hill that had served as the home of the Ottoman rulers for nearly four centuries. Dolmabahçe served as the principal imperial residence for all but one of the latter Ottoman sultans; the exception was Abdülhamit II, who preferred the more secluded palace that he built for himself a bit farther up the European shore of the Bosphorus at Yıldız. After the establishment of the Turkish Republic, Dolmabahçe served as Atatürk's presidential residence whenever he was in Istanbul. Atatürk stayed in Dolmabahçe during his last illness, and he died there on 10 November 1938, in a seaside bedroom that is still furnished as it was at the time of his death. The palace was restored in the 1960s and since then it has been open as a museum, used occasionally as a showplace for gala official functions.

The most impressive aspect of the palace is its seaside facade of gleaming white marble, 284 meters in length, with its quay extending for some 600 meters. The core of the palace is a great imperial state hall flanked by two main wings containing the state rooms and the royal apartments, with the *selamlık*, or men's quarters, on the south side and the *harem*, or women's section, on the north. The apartment of the Valide Sultan is in a separate wing linked to the Sultan's *harem* through the apartment of the Crown Prince; in addition there is another *harem* for the women of the princes, and still another residence at the northwest corner of the palace for the Chief Black Eunuch. The complex also included rooms for those of the palace staff who lived within Dolmabahçe, as well as kitchens, an *imaret* (refectory) to feed the staff, an infirmary with a pharmacy, stables, carriage houses, and barracks for the halberdiers who guarded the palace. Altogether there are 285 rooms, including 43 large *salons* and six *hamams*, with the Sultan's private bath equipped with an alabaster bath tub.

The palace interior was the work of the French decorator Sechan, who designed the Paris Opera, and thus the decor and furniture of Dolmabahçe are strongly reminiscent of French palaces and mansions of a somewhat earlier period. A number of European artists were commissioned to adorn the palace with paintings, including Boulanger, Gerome, Fromentin, Ayvasovski and Zonaro. Examples of their works can still be seen in the original rooms for which they were commissioned, and others are displayed in the Exhibition Hall, which has a separate entrance on the courtyard off the shore highway. The opulent furnishings of the palace include 4,455 square meters of hand-woven Hereke carpets; the fireplaces and chandeliers are of Bohemian glass and Baccarat crystal; and the world's largest chandelier hangs in the State Room, comprising four and one-half tons of Bohemian glass with 750 lights, a gift of Czar Nicholas II to Sultan Abdülmecit. A great showpiece is the ornate stairway that leads up from the Salon of the Ambassadors, its balusters made of Baccarat crystal and its upper level framed by monoliths of variegated marble. Two-thirds of the palace is taken up by the *harem*, the most impressive chambers of which are the Valide Sultan's apartment, the Mavi (Blue) Salon, the Pembe (Pink) Salon, the apartment of Sultan Abdülaziz, Atatürk's apartment, and the School Room.

We now continue on to Beşiktaş, whose *iskele* is the first stop for ferries going up the Bosphorus. Its name means "cradle-stone," for which Evliya gives his usual apocryphal but imaginative explanation:

This town was formerly called by the Infidels the 'cradle-stone', which is the translation of its present name. The country being yet covered with wood, a monk, called Yashka, built here a great church, and brought from Jerusalem the stone on which Christ was first washed after his birth at Jerusalem, which gave the name to the convent and place.

The Greek name of the village was actually Diplokion, the Two Columns. This name derived from a pair of lofty columns of Theban granite surmounted by crosses that were erected by the Emperor Romanus II Lecapenus (919-44), and it is possible that the distorted memory of these became Beşiktaş in Turkish times. In Byzantine times Diplokion was an important port with a royal palace and a hippodrome, along with a famous church of Ayios (Saint) Mamas. These have vanished without a trace, although there is a nineteenth-century Greek Orthodox church on the shore highway dedicated to Ayios Mamas. Beşiktaş continued to be an important port in Ottoman times, and the Turkish fleet used it as an anchorage.

There are several places of interest around the Beşiktaş İskelesi associated with the Ottoman fleet and some of its famous admirals. In the park by the *iskele* is the *türbe* of Hayrettin Paşa, the most renowned of Süleyman's admirals, better known in the West as Barbarossa, conqueror of Tunis, Tripoli, Algiers and the Aegean isles of Greece. The *türbe* is one of the earliest works of Sinan, dated by an inscription over the door to 1542, four years before the death of Barbarossa. The structure is octagonal in plan, with two rows of windows. The upper row of windows has recently been filled in with stained glass, and the dome has been rather well repainted with white arabesques on a rust-colored ground. There are three catafalques in the *türbe*, the large one in the middle being that of Barbarossa, and in the little garden outside there is a cluster of handsome sarcophagi.

On the fourth centennial of Barbarossa's death a statue was unveiled to his memory in the center of the park facing his *türbe*, a vivid and lively work by the sculptor Zühdü Müridoğlu. On the back are six verses by the celebrated poet Yahya Kemal Beyatlı (1884-1958), translated thus by Hilary Sumner-Boyd:

KABATAŞ TO BEBEK

> Whence on the sea's horizon comes that roar?
> Can it be Barbarossa now returning
> From Tunis or Algiers or from the Isles?
> Two hundred vessels ride upon the waves,
> Coming from lands the rising Crescent lights:
> O blessed ships, from what seas are ye come?

Across the avenue from Barbarossa's *türbe* is a brick and stone mosque, another work of Sinan built for one of Süleyman's admirals, Sinan Paşa. Inscriptions over the entrance portal and on the *şadırvan*, or ablution fountain, give the date of foundation as 1555; this was two years after the death of Sinan Paşa, whose *külliye* was completed under the sponsorship of his brother, the Grand Vezir Rüstem Paşa, Süleyman's son-in-law.

The mosque has its back to the avenue on its south, with its entrance approached by the arched portal to the right. The *türbe* of the *külliye* is to the right at the end of the passageway.

The mosque is preceded on its north side by a rectangular *avlu*, or courtyard, with a *şadırvan* in the center. Around the periphery of the *avlu* there is an arcade with a steeply sloping wooden penthouse roof; on three sides of the court there are arrayed the twelve cells of the *medrese*, with the north side of the mosque forming the fourth side. The north end of the mosque interior is in the form of a pseudo-narthex of five bays, the central one cross-vaulted the other four domed. The main prayer room is covered by a central dome 12.6 meters in diameter; this rests on the outer walls on the south, on square piers on the north, and on hexagonal piers on the two sides. Lateral arches springing from the two hexagonal piers divide the side wings into two square bays, each covered by small domes.

Beside the *iskele* on its downstream side is the Deniz Müzesi, or Naval Museum. In the garden of the museum there are a number of Ottoman cannon and more modern naval guns, along with cannon balls, torpedoes, anchors and other maritime memorabilia.

KABATAŞ TO BEBEK

The most important exhibit in the museum itself is the famous chart of the eastern coast of North America drawn by Piri Reis (1465-1554), the great Ottoman admiral, explorer and cartographer. The chart is from his *Kitabı Bahriye*, or Book of the Sea, the earliest Turkish nautical compendium. Elsewhere in the museum there are exhibits from all periods of Turkish naval history, ranging in date from Ottoman times up to the early Republican era. A separate building houses the museum's incomparable collection of *pazar kayık*s, the beautiful rowing barges that were used by the Sultans in travelling to and from their palaces.

A short distance beyond the Naval Museum, on the same side of the avenue, is the Resim ve Heykel Müzesi, the Painting and Sculpture Museum, exhibiting modern Turkish works of art.

In the hills above Beşiktaş there is a pretty little palace named Ihlamur Kasrı, the Linden Pavilion. This takes its name from Ihlamur Deresi, the Valley of the Lindens, the once lovely vale in which it is set. Ahmet III (1703-30) laid out gardens here which he used in his famous Tulip Festivals, celebrated annually during the time of the first full moon in April. These festivals set the tenor of the times, so that the reign of Ahmet III is known in Ottoman history as Lale Devri, the Age of Tulips, and he himself is remembered affectionately as the Tulip King. Abdülmecit erected a kiosk here early in his reign, and then in 1849-55 Nikogos Balyan built for him the pair of kiosks that constitute the present Ihlamur Kasrı. These are Maiyet Köşkü, the Kiosk of the Retinue, and Merasim Köşkü, the Ceremonial Kiosk. The palace has recently been restored, along with its gardens, and it is now open to the public as a museum.

Beşiktaş once had a famous *tekke*, or dervish monastery, now vanished. This was a *tekke* of the Mevlevi, famous in the West as the Whirling Dervishes, because of the beautiful twirling dance that they performed to the haunting music of the *ney*, or Turkish flute. Evliya writes of this *tekke* in his *Seyahatname*:

> The convent of the Mevlevi at Beşiktaş is one story high. The room

for the dancing and singing of the dervishes (*semahane*) looks toward the sea. It is covered with a curious wooden roof, which our present architects would be unable to execute. It is very high and lofty. The cells of the Fakirs on the west side and the dancing room are of nut-tree wood; three sides of the latter are enclosed with glass windows. Its Sheikh, Hasan Dede, who was more than a hundred and ten years old when he died, mounting the preaching chair (*Kuran kürsüsü*) on the days of meeting and becoming enraptured, sometimes commented upon the verses of the Mesnevi, according to the original intentions of their author [Celaladin Rumi, founder of the Mevlevi]. His successor, Nizen Dervish Yusuf Jelali, at times threw himself down from the chair on the Fakirs, and when he sang, he was in such raptures that all of those who heard him remained astonished. All divine lovers collected around him and listened to his heavenly songs until they were out of their senses. He was a Prince in the speculative sense of contemplation.

Beşiktaş and the other localities on the European shore of the lower Bosphorus have now been so amalgamated into the sprawling urban mass of Istanbul that they are no longer distinct communities as they were in times past, each with their own definite character. Evliya describes the people of Beşiktaş as they were in his day, the mid-seventeenth century:

The inhabitants of Beşiktaş are pleasant people; a great number occupy themselves with gardening. They dress in different styles. The greatest number of them are Anatolians, but there are also a number of Constantinopolitans. The fair sex of Beşiktaş are high-spirited, they look on their lovers but from the corner of their eye, and flatter no strangers. They keep their favors to their own people, and are renowned for their attachment.

Continuing up the Bosphorus, about 500 meters beyond the Beşiktaş İskelesi we pass the former Çırağan Sarayı, now the Çırağan Palace Hotel.

Çırağan was built during the reign of Abdülaziz and was completed in 1874. The Sultan died there on 4 June 1876, five days after he had been deposed. His death was officially declared to be a suicide, but the suspicious circumstances suggested to many of his contemporaries that he had been murdered. His nephew and successor, Murat V, was so mentally unstable at the time of his accession that he proved unable to rule, whereupon that same year he was deposed in favor of his brother, Abdülhamit II. (The people of Istanbul for long afterwards referred to 1876 as "the year of the three Sultans."). For the next three decades Murat and his family were kept as virtual prisoners in Çırağan, living in conditions of almost unbelievable squalor and degradation. Murat died there in 1905, after which the palace was abandoned. Then, after the creation of the Constitution of 1908, Çırağan was restored and used for a time to house the new Turkish Parliament. But then one night in January 1910 Çırağan was totally gutted in a disastrous fire, leaving only a smoke-blackened shell that was allowed to stand on the shore of the Bosphorus for the following three-quarters of a century. During the mid-1980s the present Çırağan Palace Hotel was erected on the site, using the shell of the ruined palace for part of its Bosphorus facade.

A few hundred meters beyond Çırağan the shore highway passes on its left the lower entrance to Yıldız Parkı, the site of Yıldız Sarayı, the Palace of the Star.

The gardens here, originally known as Çirağan, are first mentioned during the reign of Murat IV, who bestowed them on his daughter Kaya Sultan and her husband Melek Ahmet Paşa, his Grand Vezir. After their time the gardens reverted to the imperial family. Ahmet III gave the gardens to his son-in-law, the Grand Vezir Nevşehirli Damat İbrahim Paşa, who here hosted the Sultan and his court in some of the flamboyant fetes of the Tulip Period. The first imperial structure known to have been erected here was a pavilion built for Mihrişah Sultan, mother of Selim III, but this has long since vanished. Yıldız Sarayı first began to take form in the upper gardens during the time of Mahmut II, and the buildings that we see there today date from his reign through that of Abdülhamit II. Abdülhamit lived in Yıldız almost exclusively throughout his long and repressive reign, preferring its secluded vales to the more exposed locations of Dolmabahçe and other palaces on the shores of the Bosphorus. But this was not just a pleasure dome, for Abdülhamit, like all of the preceding Ottoman sultans, had been trained from childhood in a practical trade, that of cabinetmaking, and he set up workshops on the palace grounds to manufacture both furniture and porcelain of exceedingly high quality for Yıldız Sarayı and the other imperial palaces and pavilions along the Bosphorus. After Abdülhamit was deposed in 1909 the palace was abandoned as an imperial residence and began to deteriorate. But then in the 1970s the various pavilions of the palace and its grounds were splendidly restored by the Turkish Touring and Automobile Club, under the direction of Çelik Gülersoy, and today Yıldız Sarayı is open to the public, one of the principal adornments on the shores of the Bosphorus.

Just beside the lower gate we see on the right, Mecidiye Camii, a nondescript mosque built by one of the Balyan architects for Abdülmecit; it has a quaint but ugly minaret in a pseudo-Gothic style.

One can walk up through Yıldız Parkı by the road or, preferably, along a series of tree-shaded paths, passing through the most extensive tract of woodland remaining along the European shore of the Bosphorus. A number of kiosks and greenhouses on the palace grounds have been converted into cafés, including the Çadır Köşkü, the Lale Sera (Tulip Conservatory), the Yeşil Sera (Green Conservatory), and, most notably, the Malta Köşkü, a little palace in the upper part of the park. The setting of the garden café outside the Malta Köşkü is idyllic, with a romantic view of the Bosphorus through a dappled screen of greenery, giving one some idea of how beautiful the shores of the strait were in times past.

The most palatial of the surviving imperial residences of Yıldız Sarayı is the Şale Köşkü, so called because of its resemblance to a Swiss chalet. This consists of two buildings, the first erected in 1889 and the second in 1898; the latter is apparently the work of the Italian architect Raimondo D'Aronco, who brought to Istanbul the Art Nouveau style of architecture under the name of the Stile Floreal. The Şale Köşkü has some fifty rooms, the largest and grandest being the magnificent Reception Hall, its ceiling decorated in gold leaf, with other splendid chambers called the Mother-of-Pearl Hall and the Yellow Parlor. The Şale Köşkü was used principally as a place of residence for visiting royalty, most notably Kaiser Wilhelm II, who during his stay with Abdülhamit II in 1895 formed an alliance between Germany and the Ottoman Empire. The kiosk has also been restored and is now open as a museum.

The city of Istanbul has recently opened a new Municipality Museum just outside the upper entrance to Yıldız Parkı. The collection contains mostly works of art from the late Ottoman period, including a number of paintings depicting the Bosphorus and its shores in the latter years of the Empire.

Returning to the Bosphorus road, a few steps beyond the entrance to Yıldız Parkı a steep but short street leads up to the picturesque *külliye* of Yahya Efendi. Yahya Efendi was a foster brother of Süleyman the Magnificent, whom his mother nursed as an infant, and he became one of the most celebrated holy men in Istanbul in the sixteenth century. The little *külliye*, consisting of a *türbe* and a *medrese* built by Sinan presumably shortly before Yahya's death in 1570, is now enveloped by various wooden structures of the nineteenth century, and it is difficult to see or even to ascertain what is left of the *medrese*; its *dershane* at least appears to be intact. The *türbe* communicates by a large grilled opening to a small wooden mosque with a baroque wooden dome. The various buildings themselves are picturesque, but even more so are their surroundings, where topsy-turvy tombstones lie scattered among a lovely copse of trees, through which one catches occasional glimpses of the Bosphorus. The appearance of this place seems to have changed little across the centuries, as we gather from Evliya's description: "The walk of Yahya Efendi is in a deep shaded recess of the hills, luxuriant with plane, cypress, willow, fir, and nut trees.

Some well intentioned people have constructed a *sofa* at the foot of the spring, within the murmur of which all kinds of birds sing their melodious notes. It is an old pleasure place, where friends are wont to meet." Evliya goes on to say that "Yahya Efendi is buried on the top of a hill overlooking the sea; the four walls of his *türbe* are covered with the inscriptions of a hundred thousand divine lovers breathing out their feelings in verse. Even now he converses every Friday night with Hızır İlyas, taking from him lessons in mysticism." The place is evidently very holy, and it is always thronged with pious people at their devotions.

The next village along the Bosphorus is Ortaköy, whose *iskele* is the second stop on the European shores for ferries going up the strait. In Byzantine times this village was called Ayios Phocas, because of a famous church of that saint which stood here. There is still a Greek church of Ayios Phocas on the shore road in Ortaköy, and though the present building was erected only in 1872 the parish dates back to the Byzantine period. A block away from the shore road there is a synagogue dating from 1913, but this congregation must also be a very old one in origin, since Evliya tells us that in his time Ortaköy had large numbers of both Jewish and Greek families in addition to its Muslim Turkish population. Although Ortaköy is now part of the urban mass of Istanbul, it still has a village atmosphere about it, and many of its old wooden houses of the late Ottoman period have been restored. In recent years it has become something of a local arts and crafts centre, and a number of lively restaurants, cafés and bars have opened in the area around the *iskele*, where there is a pleasant park. The large number of drinking places in Ortaköy is in keeping with its past character, as we gather from Evliya's description of the village: "The place is full of Infidels and Jews; there are two hundred shops, a great number of which are taverns."

Evliya also mentions that Ortaköy has a *hamam* built by Sinan. This is on the left side of the shore road at the main intersection. The *hamam* was built by Sinan for Hüsrev Kethüda, who served as steward for the Grand Vezir Sokollu Mehmet Paşa in the early

KABATAŞ TO BEBEK

1570s; unfortunately there is no inscription to date the building. As so often happens, the facade on the street has been hidden by a modern stucco house-front built against it. It is a double bath, with separate establishments for men and women, the two of them virtually identical. The interior is curious and unlike any other bath by Sinan. From a *camekân* of the usual form (though confused by a modern gallery), one enters a rather large *soğukluk* consisting of a central area in two unequal bays each covered by a cradle-vault; at one end are the lavatories, at the other a bathing-cubicle. From the central area the *hararet* is entered. This, instead of being the usual large domed cruciform room, consists of four domed areas of almost equal size. The first two of these communicate with each other by a wide arch. Here, instead of the central *göbektaşı*, there is a raised marble sofa or podium against one wall, with domed bathing cubicles leading from it.

The most prominent monument in Ortaköy is Mecidiye Camii, a charming baroque mosque dramatically situated on the promontory just upstream from the ferry landing. The mosque was built for Sultan Abdülmecit in 1854 by Nikogos Balyan, architect of Dolmabahçe Camii and Dolmabahçe Palace. But Mecidiye Camii is a much better building than either of those two edifices; although the style as usual is hopelessly mixed, there is a genuinely baroque verve and movement in the undulating walls of the tympani of the great dome arches.

From Ortaköy onwards the European shore of the Bosphorus is best seen from the deck of a ferry, for the individual villages are separated from one another by appreciable distances. Just beyond Mecidiye Camii we see the ruins of what remains of the Küçük Esma Sultan Sarayı, an early seventeenth-century Ottoman palace gutted by a fire in 1975. The palace takes its name from Esma Sultan (1778-1845), a daughter of Abdülhamit I, nicknamed Küçük, or Little, to distinguish her from an older princess of the same name, a daughter of Ahmet III. Küçük Esma Sultan was given this palace as her own when she was ten years old; she was married here when she was fourteen to the statesman Hüseyin Paşa, who died eleven years later. Unlike other Ottoman princesses, who were married young and widowed early and often, Esma never remarried, but devoted the rest of her life to "pleasure, entertainment and dissipation," as Tülay Artan writes of her in *The Palaces of the Sultanas* (Istanbul Magazine, 1992). Esma Sultan exercised great power in the Ottoman court during the successive reigns of her cousin Selim II, her brother Mustafa IV (1807-08) and her stepbrother Mahmut II, whose protection gave her absolute license to indulge herself in a debauched life that shocked even jaded Istanbul. Melek Hanım, wife of the Grand Vezir Kıbrıslı Mehmet Paşa, writes of Esma Sultan in her memoirs, published in 1872:

The princess was a woman of strong passions, but, at the same time, of a most cruel disposition. She exercised great influence over her brother, Sultan Mahmut. It is related that she used to amuse herself by collecting ten young Greeks duly shaved and painted, and making them dance in female costume. On several occasions her brother, hearing of the debauches to which she gave herself up to with these dancers, had them seized and put to death, wherat his sister seemed to be not the least affected. Once while taking a walk in the country, seeing a young peasant of prepossessing appearance, she invited him to come to the palace with some flowers and other trifles. Once admitted, nothing more was ever heard of the unhappy youth; he was massacred, after having afforded a pastime to this capricious and cruel woman.

A short distance beyond the ruined palace is the Balyan Usta Yalısı, wedged in between two modern houses. The *yalı*, or seaside mansion, was built in the 1860s by the architect Sarkis Balyan, brother of Nikogos Balyan. Sarkis Balyan shifted the orientation of his *yalı* at a slight angle to the shore, doing this so that he could look directly across the Bosphorus to Beylerbeyi Sarayı, the palace that he erected for Sultan Abdülaziz in the years 1861-65.

Just beyond Ortaköy we pass under Boğaziçi Köprüsü, the first Bosphorus Bridge, which was opened on 29 October 1973, on the fiftieth anniversary of the founding of the Turkish Republic. At the time of its opening this was the fourth longest suspension bridge in the world (it is now the sixth longest), 1,074 meters in length between the two great piers on the opposing continental shores, and with its roadway 64 meters above the water at the middle of the strait.

After passing under the bridge the ferry passes Defterdar Burnu, the promontory that divides Ortaköy from the next village along the shore, Kuruçeşme. The promontory takes its name from Defterdar Camii, the old wooden mosque on the shore just beyond the point. This was built in the mid-sixteenth century by Süleyman's Defterdar Paşa, or Chief Accountant.

Ferries no longer stop at the *iskele* of Kuruçeşme, and the ferry station there has now been converted into a restaurant named the Captain's Kiosk. The name of the village means "the dried-up well." Its Greek name was Anaplous, first mentioned when the Emperor Constantine the Great (324-37) erected a church here dedicated to the Archangel Michael, which was restored in turn by Justinian the Great (527-65) and Isaac II Angelus (1185-95, 1203-04). Anaplous was also renowned for its two famous stylites, or pillar-sitting saints; Simeon the Stylite sat it out on a column here in the years 433-60, and after his death the Stylite Daniel replaced him on the same perch for the next thirty-four years, drawing huge crowds from Constantinople. Fatih demolished the church in 1452 and used its stones in the construction of Rumelihisarı. Evliya writes thus of the village, which by his time was already called Kuruçeşme:

The houses of gentlemen border upon the seashore; inland, in an extensive valley, is a quarter of Muslims, with a bath and a mosque; two congregations of Jews, and three quarters of Greeks. The Jews have three synagogues, and the Greeks two churches, and altogether there are two hundred shops. There are no visiting places of saints and no walks.

There are still an old wooden mosque and a *hamam* along the shore road in Kuruçeşme, and in the interior of the village, which

KABATAŞ TO BEBEK

Ortaköy: Mecidiye Camii with the Boğaziçi Köprüsü in the background

Arnavutköy: Arnavutköy İskelesi prior to the new coast road's construction

KABATAŞ TO BEBEK 51

climbs steeply up the hill from the Bosphorus, there are two Greek churches, one of them with an *ayazma*, or holy well. But the synagogues of which Evliya writes have vanished.

We then round a promontory and come to Arnavutköy, the Albanian Village, whose *iskele* is the third stop for ferries going up the European shore of the Bosphorus. There is a very pretty line of *yalı*s along the waterfront just upstream from the *iskele*, although the new highway that has been built in front of them somewhat spoils the view. The interior of the village is quite picturesque, the streets lined with old wooden houses of the late Ottoman era, some of them embowered with vines. Evliya tells us that in his day the village was inhabited almost entirely by Greeks and Jews, with only a few Muslims. Here again the Jewish community has vanished, but Arnavutköy still has more than fifty Greek families, who worship in the large church of the Taxiarchs at the northern end of the village. The square in front of the church and the lanes that lead off from it are the site of a popular street-market every Thursday.

On the highest hill above Arnavutköy are the buildings and grounds of Robert College, an American coeducational lycée for Turkish students, founded in 1871 as the American College for Women. This was one of the first modern secondary schools of its kind in Turkey and produced many women who played a leading part in the life of their country, the most famous being the writer Halide Edib Adıvar. In 1971, on the occasion of its centenary, the American College for Girls was amalgamated with the boys' lycée of the original Robert College, a little farther up the Bosphorus. The new institution perpetuates the name of Robert College on the grounds above Arnavutköy, from where there are superb views of the middle Bosphorus.

The promontory that separates Arnavutköy harbor from the bay of Bebek, the next village up the Bosphorus, is called Akıntı Burnu, the Cape of the Current. The Bosphorus makes a very abrupt bend here as its waters come sweeping out of the Narrows, and as a result the current off Akıntı Burnu is extremely powerful, and when the prevailing north wind is blowing the current can reach a speed of seven knots, making it difficult for small boats to round the point going upstream. In times past, sailing vessels making their way up the strait often had to be towed around this point by porters on shore. Apparently crabs also found it difficult, and leaving the water walked overland across the point, for Gyllius, after quoting Dionysius Byzantius and Aelian in his support, says: "I myself saw there stones worn down by the long procession of crabs. And even if I had not seen it, I should not have thought it far from the truth that stones should be worn down by the hard claws of crabs, since we see that ants can dig out furrows and make a path by the continuous attrition of their feet."

After rounding Akıntı Burnu the ferry enters Bebek Bay, one of the most beautiful havens on the Bosphorus. Lush rolling hills with groves of umbrella pines and cypresses rise up to form a verdant background to the bay, particularly along its southern shore, where the woods known as Kortel Korusu still preserve their natural beauty, almost totally untouched by modern housing developments. As the ferry approaches the *iskele* it passes the Egyptian Embassy, built around the turn of the nineteenth-twentieth century by the Italian architect Raimondo D'Aronco. At the water's edge just past the *iskele* there is a little mosque built in 1913 by Kemalettin Bey, a leader of the neo-classical school of Turkish architecture. Like most of Kemalettin Bey's buildings, it is a little lifeless and dull, although the setting is quite pretty. Bebek itself was once one of the most beautiful communities on the Bosphorus, but it has been somewhat spoiled by the proliferation of modern apartment houses and high-priced restaurants and cafés, giving it the atmosphere of a resort town instead of the fishing village that it was still within living memory. A few of the old fishermen still keep their boats moored along the quay just north of the village center in Küçük Bebek. The dean of the Bebek fishermen is Rıza Kaptan, a Romanian Turk who fought in the Turkish War of Independence and then settled in Bebek in 1923, building the little wooden *iskele* where he has been working on his boat and his fishing gear ever since, still handsome and vigorous as he approaches his ninetieth year, rising to his feet with a smile to greet old friends passing along the quay. This is the Bebek that was, and which will be only a memory when Rıza goes.

Bebek: Bebek Camii

Bebek: Egyptian Consulate

Bebek: a Bosphorus view from above Bebek

CHAPTER FOUR
BEBEK TO RUMELİHİSARI

Bebek is a good base from which to stroll along the European shore of the middle Bosphorus, for the seaside promenade now extends all the way to Rumelihisarı, the next village, where the *iskele* is no longer used by the Bosphorus ferries. After exploring Rumelihisarı and its great fortress, one can walk back along the quay to the *iskele* in Bebek, from where one can then travel up the Bosphorus by ferry to Rumelikavağı, the last stop on the European side, perhaps breaking the voyage at other *iskele*s along the way.

As we walk along the quay in Bebek we see on the left side of the shore highway an old wooden house with an archway in its middle. This is the beginning of what is known as the "twisty-turney" road leading up to Bogaziçi Üniversitesi, the University of the Bosphorus, whose buildings and grounds are on the hilltop between Bebek and Rumelihisarı. This Turkish university was founded in 1971, occupying the buildings and grounds of the old Robert College. Robert College, which in its time was the finest institution of higher education in Turkey, was founded in 1863 by Cyrus Hamlin, an American missionary who had baked bread and washed clothes for Florence Nightingale while she was running her hospital in Üsküdar during the Crimean War. The College was named after Christopher Robert, an American philanthropist who provided the initial funds to build and run the institution. During its early years the students at the College were all Christian minorities of the Ottoman Empire - Armenians, Greeks and Bulgars - with the first Turk, the distinguished Hüseyin Pektaş, graduating in 1908. Thereafter the percentage of ethnic Turks increased rapidly, and by the time the College celebrated its centennial they were the predominant majority, with the rest of the student body

56 BEBEK TO RUMELİHİSARI

Bebec on the Bosphorus

Turkish Country House on the Bosphorus

BEBEK TO RUMELİHİSARI 57

made up mostly of Greek, Armenian and Jewish citizens of Turkey. About half of the faculty members were Turkish and the other half mostly American, along with some Europeans, with an American President and a Turkish Vice-President. Then in 1971 the administration of the institution was transferred to the Turkish government, which created the new University of the Bosphorus, whose first graduates received their degrees in June 1972. Since then the university has expanded to a new campus higher up the hill, its student body now numbering 8,000, ten times that of Robert College in its later years. During the 108 years of its existence the College had among its staff and graduates a number of important men (it was coeducational only in its last decade), including several who played a leading role in the cultural and political life of Turkey, as well as of Bulgaria and Greece. It produced one Prime Minister of Turkey - Bülent Ecevit, a graduate of the class of 1951 - and one of its former faculty members, Erdal İnönü, became Associate Prime Minister in 1992. The terrace on the old campus commands a superb view of the middle Bosphorus framed in the towers of Rumelihisarı.

Continuing along the shore road, we pass Arifi Paşa Korusu; then just beyond we see a little wooden mosque named Kâtip Camii, dating from the eighteenth century, and beside it a small graveyard with a few turbaned tombstones. A little way farther along we see above on a retaining wall the Yılanlı Yalı, the House of Snakes. This is a modern replica of the original Yılanlı Yalı, built in the mid-eighteenth century and destroyed by fire in the mid-1960s. One of its first owners was Mustafa Efendi, Chief of the Royal Secretariat in the reign of Mustafa III (1757-74). One day the Sultan, who was known to covet and confiscate beautiful houses, was passing along the Bosphorus in his caique when he stopped to admire the *yalı* here, asking his chief boatmen to tell him what he knew of it. The boatman, who was a good friend of Mustafa Efendi, said that the *yalı*, though well-built, was uninhabitable because it was infested with snakes. "How unfortunate!" said the Sultan with a sigh, whereupon he told his boatman to row on, or so the story goes, and thenceforth the house was known as the Yılanlı Yalı.

We then come to the promontory at Aşiyan, which is the boundary between Bebek and Rumelihisarı. Aşiyan means "The Nest," taking its name from the house of Tevfik Fikret (1867-1915), which is approached by the road that leads uphill past the cemetery, turning off to the left just before the top. Aşiyan is now a museum, its exhibits memorabilia of the life and works of Tevfik Fikret, who was for many years professor of Turkish Literature at Robert College. He was one of the leading poets of his time, an idealist and utopian socialist who was convinced that the salvation of Turkey lay in its youth.

At the foot of the Aşiyan hill a pretty park has recently been laid out beside the Bosphorus road. In the center of the park there is a bronze statue of the Turkish poet Orhan Veli (1914-50), who is shown feeding several sea birds, which he was wont to do while sitting on the shore of the Bosphorus as represented in his memorial here. Seeing him like this, one is reminded of one of his poems - "Something's Up!" - translated thus by David Garwood:

> Is the sea this lovely every day?
> Do the skies look like this all the time,
> Are things, this window, for instance, always as lovely as this?
> No, certainly not,
> I swear it.
> There's something behind all this beauty

Orhan Veli is buried across the road in the Kayalar Mezarlığı, the huge Turkish cemetery that stretches along the Bosphorus as far as the fortress walls of Rumelihisarı, extending up to the top of the hill above. This is one of the two oldest Muslim burial grounds on the European side of Istanbul, the other being on the hill above the village of Rumelihisarı, both of them dating back to the Turkish Conquest. H. G. Dwight gives an evocative description of the cemetery in his *Constantinople, Settings and Traits*,

BEBEK TO RUMELİHİSARI 59

published in 1926, where he reminisces about the Rumelihisarı of times long past:

Another memento of that older time is to be seen in the cemetery lying under the castle wall to the south. It is perhaps the oldest Mohammedan burying ground in Constantinople or at least on the European shore of the Bosphorus. It certainly is the most romantic, with its jutting rocks, its ragged black cypresses, its round tower and crenellated wall, overhanging a blue so fancifully cut by Asiatic hills. It has too, a spicy odor quite its own, an odor compounded of thyme, of resinous woods, of sea-salt, and I know not what aroma of antiquity. But its most precious characteristic is the grave information it shares with other Mohammedan cemeteries. There is nothing about it to remind one of conventional mourning, no alignment of tombs, no rectilinear laying out of walks, no trim landscape gardening. It lies unwalled to the world, the gravestones scattered as irregularly on the steep hillside as the cyclamens that blossom there in February. Many of them have the same brightness of color. The tall narrow slabs are often painted, with the decorative Arabic lettering, or some quaint floral design, picked out in gold. It is another expression of the guardhouse soldiers who so often lounge along the water, of the boy who plays his pipe under a cypress while the village goats nibble among the graves, of the veiled women who preen their silks among the rocks on summer afternoons. The whole place is interfused with that intimacy of life and death, the sense of which makes the Asiatic so much more mature than the European. The one takes the world as he finds it, while the other must childlessly beat his head against stone walls; it is the source of the strength and of the weakness of the two stocks.

The shore road divides at the foot of the Aşiyan hill, and we follow its upper part along the lower wall of the cemetery, which ends when we come to the southern sea tower of the great fortress of Rumelihisarı. At that point a stairway leads up into the cemetery, where up against the fortress wall we find the tombstone of Durmuş Dede, a famous Muslim divine who founded a dervish *tekke* here early in the seventeenth century, and who was buried here in 1648. The *tekke* was closed when the dervish orders were banned in the early years of the Republic. It was then demolished in 1936, when work began on the present Bosphorus road, which is laid out on filled-in land. Before that time boats going up the European shore of the Bosphorus passed right underneath the walls of the fortress, and up until late Ottoman times sailors would drop off food and wood for the dervishes in the *tekke*, for they believed that Durmuş Dede would then give them good luck on their voyage. The tombstones of a number of the dervishes who dwelt in the *tekke* can be seen around the grave of Durmuş Dede. Among those buried here is Sheikh İsmail Çelebi, who was executed along with ten of his disciples during the reign of Murat IV. Evliya Çelebi tells the story of how the Sheikh and his followers miraculously came to their final resting place here:

Sheikh İsmail Çelebi and ten of his disciples were executed at the Hippodrome; their bodies were thrown into the sea at the Stable Gate, from where they miraculously floated up the Bosphorus against the current. The Emperor [Murat IV] was then at Kandilli [on the Asian shore opposite Bebek] when he saw the remains of the Sheikh and his ten followers floating by, dancing on the waves with their heads in their hands. The Emperor's suite seeing this miracle, represented to him that they must have been unjustly executed. The Emperor began to weep as he watched them floating against the current to the opposite shore of Rumelihisarı, where they were buried at the foot of Durmuş Dede, and where, during ten nights, light was seen pouring down on their graves.

We now pass below the walls of Rumelihisarı, whose entrance is just beyond the sea tower of Halil Paşa and its protecting barbican.

The story of this great fortress, the mightiest ever erected by the Ottoman Turks, begins in 1451, when the young Mehmet II succeeded as Sultan on the death of his father, Murat II. (Murat had twice before retired in favor of Mehmet, but on both occasions his son had proved unready for the task and so he had returned to the throne.). Two years before that Constantine XI (1449-

The Castles of Europe and Asia

Rumelihisarı

53) succeeded to the throne in Constantinople, fated to be the last Emperor of Byzantium. The year after he became Sultan Mehmet began preparations for the long-awaited siege of Constantinople, which his great grandfather Beyazit I had besieged unsuccessfully in the years 1394-1402, building a fortress on the Bosphorus at Anadoluhisarı. Mehmet's first step was to cut off the city from its sources of grain on the Anatolian coast of the Black Sea, and so he decided to build a fortress opposite Anadoluhisarı, thereby controlling the strait at its narrowest point. He demanded from Constantine a plot of land on which to build his fortress, and the Emperor was powerless to disagree. The Sultan himself selected the site, drew the general plan of the fortress, and hired a thousand artisans and two thousand laborers for the task, which began in April 1452. He entrusted the construction of each of the three main towers of the fortress to one of his vezirs: the north tower to Saruca Paşa, the south tower to Zağanos Paşa, and the sea tower to Halil Paşa, his Grand Vezir. The three of them strove to complete their task with the greatest speed and efficiency, while Mehmet himself assumed the overall supervision of the project, which was completed in August of that same year, less than four months after it was started. The castle was then garrisoned with a force of Janissaries, whose bombardiers trained their huge cannon on the strait, as warnings were delivered to all foreign powers not to send shipping through the Bosphorus. One Venetian captain made the attempt but his ship was sunk by the Turkish artillery, after which he and his surviving crew members were executed by impalement. Constantinople was thus cut off from the Black Sea, an important factor in its fall to Fatih's besieging army on 29 May 1453. After the Conquest the fortress lost its military importance and it became a mere garrison post and prison, particularly for foreign ambassadors and prisoners of war. A small village developed within the walls of Rumelihisarı, inhabited by the soldiers of the garrison and their families, but this was demolished when the fortress was restored in preparation for the celebration of the five-hundredth anniversary of the Turkish conquest of Constantinople in 1953. The fortress was then converted into a museum, and to-

BEBEK TO RUMELİHİSARI 63

day it is also used during the summer for theatrical performances associated with the Istanbul Festival.

The fortress spans a deep valley with two tall towers on opposite hills and a third at the bottom of the valley by the Bosphorus road, where there is a sea gate protected by a barbican. A curtain wall, defended by three smaller towers, joins the three major ones, forming an irregular figure some 250 meters long by 125 meters broad at its maximum. The north tower, built by Zağanos Paşa, was used as a prison in Ottoman times, and includes a small museum showing objects used by the Janissaries. The area inside the fortress has been made into a park, and the circular cistern on what once stood a small mosque (part of the minaret has been left to mark its position) has been converted into the acting area of a Greek-type theater. In and around the fortress there are a number of old Ottoman cannon dating from the time of the Conquest.

Continuing along the Bosphorus road past the sea walls of the fortress, we come to the little brick and stone mosque of Hacı Kemalettin. An inscription over the entrance records that the mosque was first built by a Hacı Kemalettin, and that it was later restored by Mahmut I in 1743. The historian İnciciyan, writing in 1794, was of the opinion that this mosque dated back to the time of Mehmet the Conqueror.

This brings us to the village of Rumelihisarı, one of the most picturesque communities on the Bosphorus, set at the narrowest part of the strait just north of the great fortress, around whose walls its higher houses cluster. The village dates back to the time of the Conquest, or possibly a year or two before, when a Bektaşi dervish *tekke* was founded on the top of the hill above, a place known as Evliyalar, or the Saints. The history and monuments of the village are described in an excellent little book by İhsan Kesedar, the former *muhtar* (mayor) of Rumelihisari, first published in 1963 and reissued along with an English translation in 1983. İhsan Bey writes of the ethnic composition of the village as it was half a century ago:

In the 1940s there were about 110 Armenian and 300 Turkish families in

Rumelihisarı: Hacı Kemalettin Camii

the village. There were also five or six Greek families - one was a butcher's family, three were grocers. The Muslim Turks were mostly civil servants, seamen, fishermen or farmers, some worked for Robert College. As for the Armenians, most worked at Robert College or for the Americans resident in Istanbul. There were also some Armenians who were fishermen, craftsmen, or small tradesmen in town.

The focal point of Rumelihisarı is the little seaside square where the main street of the village joins the area around the *iskele*, which, unfortunately, is no longer used by the Bosphorus ferries and has recently been converted into a bar. Old prints and paintings show how picturesque the area around the *iskele* was in times past, when the market was located here along with several coffeehouses and cafés. Dwight writes nostalgically of this vanished scene:

...the true centre of our municipal life is the charshi, or marketplace... My admiration is always divided between that crooked street of it, darkened by jutting upper stories that sometimes actually jump across it, wherein are situated the principal shops, the minor cafés, a fountain or two, and the public bath, and that adjoining part of it which lies open to the sea. The latter certainly offers the most facilities for the enjoyment of life. Indeed, one end of it is chiefly given up to a Company for the Promotion of Happiness - if one may so translate its Turkish name - whose English steamers carry us to town, seven miles away, or to the upper Bosphorus, as quickly, as regularly, and as comfortably as any company I know. It also does much to promote the happiness of those who do not travel, through the sociable employees of its wharf and by affording a picturesque *va et vient* at almost any hour of the day.... The boatmen, and others with them, often prefer to wait in certain agreeable resorts along that same wooden platform. The first of these is the cafe of the Armenian, whose corner rakes the Company for the Promotion of Happiness. He profits there by not a little, for when we take a steamer we do not always trouble ourselves to look up the time beforehand. The Armenian

BEBEK TO RUMELİHİSARI

is also a barber, and in his low ceilinged room of many windows, you may hear, to the accompaniment of banging backgammon boards, the choicest of conversation. The only thing I have against him is that I have to pay twice as much for my coffee as a customer who wears a girdle and a fez.

Dwight then goes on to describe the seaside square in Rumelihisarı, whose serenity has now been destroyed by the incessant traffic along the shore road:

It is not a square in any geometric sense. It is a broad stone quay of irregular width - tree shaded, awning-hung, festooned with vines and fishnets - adorned by a flat topped fountain whose benches are a superior place of contemplation, bordered by a quaintly broken architecture of shops, cafes and dwellings, and watched upon by a high white minaret. It is not subject to the intermittent bustle of the Company for the Promotion of Happiness, but carries on its more deliberate and more picturesque activities. Here commerce goes forward, both settled and itinerant, with loud and leisurely bargaining. Here the *kantarcı* exercises his function of weighing the freights unloaded by the picture-book boats at the quay. The headquarters of one of them is here, in a deep arch over the water. This is the bazaar caique, that goes early in the morning to the Golden Horn for the transport of such freight and passengers as do not care to patronize the more expensive Company for the Promotion of Happiness - a huge rowboat with an incurving beak and high stern, to pull whose oars the rowers drop from their feet to their backs.... Altogether a man might spend his days in that square and be the better for it. As a matter of fact, a surprising number of us find it possible to do so, sipping coffee, smoking cigarettes or waterpipes, and watching life slip by on the strong blue current of the Bosphorus.

The only old building that has survived of those that once stood along the waterfront on the seaside square by the *iskele* is Ali Pertek Camii, the stone mosque to the right of the main street running uphill from the Bosphorus road. This was built in the first

BEBEK TO RUMELİHİSARI 67

half of the seventeenth century by Pertek Ali Bey, an admiral in the reign of Murat IV. The fountain beside the mosque was built in the first half of the eighteenth century in memory of İbrahim Paşa, the father of Rakım Paşa, one of the vezirs of Mahmut I.

The street beside the mosque has been the main thoroughfare of Rumelihisarı since the time of the Conquest, leading up from the Bosphorus to the upper part of the village above the fortress. There we come to the upper *meydan*, or village square, which is behind the Saruca Paşa tower of the fortress. At the upper side of the meydan is the approach to the Istanbul International Community School, originally the Robert College Community School. The school was formerly located in the house of the Grosvenor family, founders of the National Geographic Magazine, but this was destroyed by fire in the mid-1980s. Edwin A. Grosvenor lived in this house when he wrote his two-volume work, *Constantinople,* published in 1896, the first book on the city to be illustrated extensively with photographs, some of which show Rumelihisarı as it was in the late nineteenth century. The distinctive Ottoman building at the lower part of the *meydan* to the north of the Saruca Paşa tower is the former library of Ahmet Vefik Paşa, Grand Vezir in the reign of Abdülhamit II. Grosvenor writes affectionately of the Pasha, who died in 1890 after a life spent in the service of his nation:

In the death, three years ago, of his Highness Achmet Vefik Pasha, twice Grand Vezir, former ambassador to Teheran, Paris, and St. Petersburg, at times governor of the largest and most important provinces, the village lost its most eminent inhabitant, and the Empire a patriotic and distinguished subject. A polyglot in speech, possessed of wide and varied learning, simple and unaffected as a child despite the courtliness and dignity of his bearing, the soul of honor, a statesman without fear and without reproach, scrupulously faithful to the requirements of his Mussulman creed, while most tolerant of the beliefs, and even of the prejudices, of other men of the world, he would have been an honor to any race, and embodied all that was best in his own. I recall gratefully the many hours I have passed under his hospitable roof, and pay my reverent tribute to his memory.

Ahmet Vefik Paşa sold part of his estate to Cyrus Hamlin, who established Robert College on those grounds, now the lower campus of the University of the Bosphorus. Sultan Abdülhamit II never forgave Ahmet Vefik for this, though he twice appointed him Grand Vezir. When the Paşa died the Sultan said bitterly to a confidante: 'Ahmet Vefik Pasa should be buried at the Kayalar Cemetery, where his soul would be tormented by the bells of the Christian school built on the land he sold.'

A road at the upper end of the *meydan*, Fenerli Türbe Sokağı, leads to the top of the hill above Rumelihisarı, where the vast new village of Hisarüstü has developed in the past three decades. At the top of the hill is the ancient Muslim burial-place called Evliyalar Tepesi - the Hill of the Saints - also known as Şehitlik, the Place of Martyrs. A Muslim tombstone has been found here bearing the date 1451, the year that Murat I died and Mehmet II succeeded to the throne. The top of the stone is carved in the form of an Elifi turban of the Bektaşi dervishes, who are known to have built a *tekke* here a year or two before the Conquest. According to tradition, the earliest burials here include some of Fatih's Janissaries who died in the construction of Rumelihisarı, and for that reason it is called the Place of the Martyrs. The Evliyalar from whom the cemetery takes its other name are the sainted dervishes who inhabited the Bektaşi *tekke* here. The original *tekke* from Fatih's time was destroyed in the first half of the nineteenth century, to be replaced by a wooden structure that remained standing until 1945. One of the most famous of the saints who lived here was Nafi Baba, who was the Sheikh of the Bektaşi brotherhood in the *tekke* during the last years of the Ottoman Empire. Nafi Baba was succeeded by his son Nüshed Baba, who was Sheikh up until the time that the tekke was suppressed in the early years of the Turkish republic, after which he emigrated to the United States. Nüshed Baba returned for a last visit to the site of the ancient *tekke* in

BEBEK TO RUMELİHİSARI

1968, when all of the surviving dervishes who had once lived there joined him in a farewell picnic in the graveyard around the *türbe* of Nafi Baba. The author of the present guide had the great privilege of being invited to this reunion, where he met Nüshed Baba and heard him reminisce of what life was like here in another and more serene age, when this was in fact the Hill of the Saints. Dwight also writes of this enchanting spot, which still gives one the profound feeling of being a holy place.

We also love to congregate, or in Empedoclean moods to muse alone, about another old cemetery. There on top of the steep slope above the castle, you will often see a row of women, like love-birds contemplating the universe, or a grave family picnic. There too, especially on moonlit nights, you will not seldom hear voices uplifted in the passionate minor key which has so compelling a charm for those who know it of old, accompanied perhaps by an oboe and the strangely broken rhythm of two little drums. It is the true music for a hilltop that is called the Place of Martyrs.... You may sit upon that hilltop in evening light and drink melancholy like an intoxication, musing upon all the change and indifference of the world. Yet life lingers there still - life that neither indifference nor change, nor time nor ruin nor death can ever quite stamp out....

A park and belvedere have now been built on the peak of the hill above Rumelihisarı. From there one can look across this most beautiful stretch of the strait, now spanned by the Fatih Sultan Mehmet Köprüsü, the Bridge of Sultan Mehmet the Conqueror, which opened in the summer of 1988. This is the fifth longest suspension bridge in the world, 1,090 meters in length between its two great piers on the facing continental shores, its roadway 64 meters above the water at the center of the strait.

The new bridge crosses the strait at what is believed to be the same place where Mandrocles of Samos built a pontoon bridge for the Persian King Darius in 512 BC, the first definite date in Bosphorean history. This historic event is described by Herodotus in Book Four of his *Histories,* where he first tells of how Darius marched his army from Susa to the Bosphorus "where the bridge was, and then took ship and sailed to the Cyanean rocks - those rocks which according to the Greek theory used to be constantly changing their position. Here, seated in the temple which stands by the straits, he looked out over the Black Sea, a sight indeed worth seeing." Then, after describing the topography of the straits, Herodotus goes on with his story:

When he had looked on the waters of the Black Sea, Darius returned by ship to the bridge, which had been designed by a Samian named Mandrocles. Then, after seeing what he could of the Bosphorus, he had two marble columns erected, on one of which was an inscription in Assyrian characters showing the various nations which were serving on the campaign; the other had a similar inscription in Greek. These nations were, in fact, all over which he had dominion, and made a total force, including cavalry but excluding the naval contingent, of 700,000 men. There were 600 ships. Years afterwards the people of Byzantium removed these columns and used them in their own city to build the altar of Artemis the Protector; a single plinth, however, covered with Assyrian characters, was left lying near the temple of Dionysus. I imagine, though I do not know for certain, that Darius' bridge was halfway between Byzantium and the temple which stands on the strait between the Bosphorus and the Black Sea.

Darius was so pleased with the bridge that he loaded its designer with presents, and Mandrocles spent a certain portion of what he received in having a picture painted, showing the whole process of the bridging of the strait, and Darius himself sitting on his throne, with the army crossing over. This picture he presented as a dedicatory offering to the temple of Hera, with the following verses inscribed upon it, to serve as a permanent record of his achievement:

> Goddess, accept this gift from Mandrocles,
> Who bridged the Bosphorus' fish-haunted seas,

BEBEK TO RUMELİHİSARI

> His labor, praised by King Darius, won
> Honor for Samos, for himself a crown.

After leaving the belvedere we make our way back down to the *meydan*, where we turn right on Ahmet Ağa Sokağı and then left on Kale Ağası Sokağı. The latter street is a country lane that leads down into the hollow between the Saruca Paşa and Zağanos Paşa towers of Rumelihisarı. This is one of the most beautiful spots on the Bosphorus, which we here see framed between the two great towers of the fortress, with a little hamlet of old Ottoman wooden houses still standing among their kitchen gardens and fruit trees, a scene reminiscent of those depicted in prints of the early nineteenth century.

At the top of the hill we turn left at the Zağanos Paşa tower and go downhill on the Aşiyan road, passing the Kayalar Cemetery on the way. We then turn right on the Bosphorus road, which we follow back to the *iskele* at Bebek, ending this excursion on the European shore of the middle Bosphorus.

Fatih Sultan Mehmet Köprüsü

CHAPTER FIVE
RUMELİHİSARI TO RUMELİKAVAĞI

After leaving Bebek the ferry rounds the promontory at Aşiyan and passes under the walls of the fortress of Rumelihisarı, after which it goes beneath the great arc of the Fatih Sultan Mehmet Bridge on its way through the Narrows.

As we pass under the bridge we see on the European shore the palace of İmer Faruk Efendi, a huge edifice dating from the late nineteenth century. The palace was built by Tophane Müşiri Zeki Paşa. It was later purchased for Prince İmer Faruk Efendi, grandson of Sultan Abdülaziz, and his wife Sabiha Sultan, daughter of Mehmet VI Vahdettin (1918-22), the last Ottoman sultan. When the Sultanate was abolished in 1922 Mehmet VI stayed in this palace during his last few days in Istanbul, and it was from here that he left Turkey on a British warship, never to return.

The next village beyond Rumelihisarı is Baltalimanı. As we approach the village we see the former palace of Ferid Paşa, Grand Vezir and son-in-law of Abdülhamit II. This palace was built in the early nineteenth century by Mustafa Reşit Paşa, Grand Vezir of Sultan Abdülmecit and founder of the Tanzimat, or Ottoman Reform movement. It was here that the Treaty of Baltalimanı was signed in 1849 between the Ottoman Empire and Russia. The palace now serves as a hospital.

Baltalimanı, the Harbor of the Axe, is named after Balta Oğlu (Son of the Axe), who commanded Fatih's fleet in the siege of Constantinople in 1453. Balta Oğlu received this name from the forest of trees he had his men chop down to build a fleet here in preparation for the siege, and which Fatih eventually had dragged across the heights of Galata to get them into the Golden Horn, a feat that contributed significantly to the Turkish victory. The Baltalimanı creek was once one of the prettiest places on the Eu-

Baltalimanı: *Yalı*s above the coast road

Emirgân: Şerifler Yalısı

ropean shore of the Bosphorus, flanked by meadows and groves of poplars, but now it has been utterly spoiled by pollution.

The ferry then stops at the *iskele* in Emirgân. The name of the village comes from the Persian prince Emirgüne, who in 1638 surrendered Erivan to Murat IV without a struggle. Emirgüne was brought back to Istanbul by Murat and became one of the Sultan's favorites in drinking and debauchery, for which he was rewarded with a seaside palace in this village. Evliya Çelebi, who was also one of Murat's favorites, gives a lyrical description of the Palace of Emirgüne in Emirgân:"'The palace is all in the Persian manner. The bath is surrounded on four sides with windows, on the outside of which roses are blooming and nightingales feeding their young. Under the shade of the trees in the garden lovers delight in taking the airs."

Along the shore road a short distance south of the *iskele* we see an Ottoman mansion with its seaward wing projecting over the garden wall on corbels. This is the Şerifler Yalısı, so called because it was rebuilt in the nineteenth century by a Şerif of Mecca named Abdullah Paşa. The *yalı* is believed to stand on the site of the Palace of Emirgüne; it was restored in the 1980s and can be visited on request.

The seaside village square in Emirgân is very picturesque, with outdoor cafés and teahouses shaded by giant plane trees. Beside the square stands a baroque mosque, partly of wood, built in 1781-82 for Abdülhamit I. The prayer room is a large rectangular chamber, almost square, but curiously asymmetrical, the decor quite elegant in its baroque way.

Just above the village are the famous tulip gardens of Emirgân, which are at their most beautiful during the annual Tulip Festival in April. The Turkish Touring and Automobile Club has in recent years restored a number of late Ottoman kiosks in the gardens, converting one of them, the Beyaz (White) Köşk, into a concert hall and others into cafes, making this a very pleasant place for an excursion.

A short distance north of the village square is the Sabancı

Emirgân: View of the *çeşme* from the mosque

mansion, built in the last years of the Ottoman period by İsmail Paşa, the Khedive of Egypt.

The next village beyond Emirgân is İstinye, which is situated on a deeply indented bay, with the *iskele* on the northern promontory. Gyllius writes of İstinye that "after the Golden Horn it must be acknowledged the largest bay and the safest port of the entire Bosphorus, rich as this is in bays and ports." Up until 1990 İstinye had the largest shipyard on the Bosphorus, with two huge floating dry-docks, but these facilities have been removed and a program of restoration is underway to recreate the natural beauty of this ancient port, which is quite picturesque with its colorful fish market along the quay.

The Turkish name İstinye is a corruption of the Greek Sosthenion; according to one version of the legend Jason and the Argonauts erected a statue here, in thanksgiving (in Greek, *sosthenion*) for aid given by a winged genius of the place against their fierce enemy on the opposite shore of the Bosphorus, King Amycus, ruler of the savage Bebryces. During the Byzantine era the name of the village was shortened to Stenos. Constantine the Great built a church here dedicated to the Archangel Michael. Stenos also had a monastery dedicated to Ayios Phocas and an imperial palace, which was destroyed by the Bulgars when they attacked Constantinople in 921 under their Tzar Symeon, only to be driven off by the Byzantine forces under Romanus I Lecapenus. In 941 the Russians made a raid down the Bosphorus and destroyed a number of villages, including Stenos, demolishing its churches, monasteries and palace and massacring all of its inhabitants. The Russians were finally driven out by the Byzantine navy, which burned many of their ships with the dread "Greek fire," a secret weapon that was a medieval precursor of the flame thrower.

Evliya describes İstinye as it was in the mid-seventeenth century:

In the time of the Infidels it was a place of convents and churches, the ruins of which even now are to be seen.... This village on the Bosphorus

RUMELİHİSARI TO RUMELİKAVAĞI

İstinye

Yeniköy: *Yalı*s

is a place of about a thousand houses, situated on the western shore of a gulf capable of containing a thousand ships. It has three mosques, seven *mescit*s [small mosques], one bath and twenty shops, no *han*s [warehouses], but many gardens. The inhabitants subsist by gardening and fishing. The air of this place is not good, owing to its being so completely landlocked. On the point is a fine kiosk, which serves for the reception of guests. In the winter two or three hundred ships ride here in safety.

At İstinye a highway leads inland to Levent, the suburb that occupies the heights above the European shore of the middle Bosphorus. A signpost on the upper highway in Levent directs one to Maslak Kasrı, an imperial Ottoman lodge originally set in spacious parklands with a view of the upper Bosphorus and its entrance from the Black Sea. Maslak Kasrı is built on a site first used as a country retreat during the reign of Mahmut II, though the present buildings appear to date mainly from the time of Abdülaziz. The various buildings of Maslak Kasrı, which has recently been restored and opened to the public, are the Kasrı Hümayun, or Imperial Lodge, which is now a museum; the Mabeyni Hümayun, or State Hall, which serves as a conservatory; the Çadır Pavilion, used as a café and bookshop; and the Paşalar Dairesi, or Pasha's Quarters, which houses the administrative staff of the complex. One apartment of especial historic interest is the privy suite used by the future Abdülhamit II when he was Crown Prince, for he was in residence here in 1876 when he received word that he had succeeded to the throne.

After leaving the *iskele* at İstinye the ferry rounds the promontory to its north, beyond which we see the stately Arif Paşa Yalısı, an Ottoman mansion of the nineteenth century.

The next village is Yeniköy, where the ferry passes the Sait Halim Paşa Yalısı before coming to the *iskele*. This was originally built in the years 1770-80 by Aristarkis, the last Logothete, or secular head of the Greek community in Istanbul. At the end of the nineteenth century it was acquired by Sait Halim Paşa, who commissioned the master builder Papa Khalfa to reconstruct it, with the first floor serving as the *harem* and the second as the *selamlık*. The *yalı* was restored in the early 1980s. There are a number of other impressive *yalı*s beyond this, most notably the Faik and Bekir Bey Yalısı, and the old Iranian summer embassy.

Yeniköy, the New Town, was known to the Byzantines as Neapolis, which has the same meaning as the Turkish name. The Greeks also called it Comarodes, from the numerous strawberries (in Greek, *coumara*), which were gathered there. Evliya tells us that the village was rebuilt by Süleyman the Magnificent:

Yeniköy is so called because it was built by Süleyman's order; it is a nice new town, consisting of three thousand houses with gardens. Its Naib is subordinate to the Molla of Trebizond; there is also an officer of Janissaries and chaushes, because the inhabitants, mostly from Trebizond, are a quarrelsome people. They are rich captains of merchant ships, and have therefore fine houses. There are three quarters of Muslims, seven of Infidels, but none of Jews, and three mosques, of which that of Kapudan Khalil Pasa on the shore is a very pleasant one. Before the house of Hacı İmer is the market of venison, that is to say of the boars and stags, which the hunters of the Janissaries take in the mountains of Istranija, and sell here in hams; they feed these animals previously to killing them in the meadow before the house of Hacı İmer. On the shore are a hundred houses of biscuit makers, for the ships that navigate the Black Sea all take their biscuits from Galata and this place. The wine is praised by debauchees, but it is indeed bad. There is no school, bedesten or fort here, but a great number of fusileers, because it happened once on the feast of Bayram that three hundred ships of Cossacks carried off a thousand prisoners and five richly laden ships. Since that time Sultan Murat IV garrisoned it with a company of Janissaries, and ordered the Bostancıbaşı to keep watch throughout the night.

There is still a substantial community of Greeks resident in Yeniköy; their parish church, dedicated to Ayios Yiorgios (St. George), has an old graveyard in which three Ecumenical Patriarchs of the Greek Orthodox Church are buried. Their other church, dedicated to the Virgin, has an ancient sacred icon of the Panayia Commariotisa, Our Lady of Comarodes, referring to the old Greek name of the village. There is also a large Armenian Catholic church on the heights at the northern end of the village. At the northern extremity of the village on the shore is the summer residence of the old embassy of Austria-Hungary, now the Austrian summer consulate.

After leaving Yeniköy the ferry passes the hamlet of Kalender, named after the mendicant order of dervishes who had a *tekke* here in Ottoman times. The first prominent building we see along the shore is the Kalender Köşkü, an imperial summer pavilion rebuilt in stone by Sultan Abdülaziz. It is now part of a Turkish Officers' Club. Farther along is the huge white Presidential Palace. This was built in late Ottoman times by a German family named Haber; in the 1980s it was requisitioned by President Kenan Evren for use as a summer residence for the President of Turkey. Beyond that is the old German summer embassy, a nineteenth-century *yalı* presented to Kaiser Wilhelm II by Abdülhamit II. The *yalı* now serves as the German summer consulate.

We now pass Tarabya, whose *iskele* is no longer used by the Bosphorus ferries. The crescent-shaped bay of Tarabya has long been celebrated as the most beautiful on the Bosphorus, but the village itself has lost most of its former charm, lined with expensive restaurants and with a luxury hotel dominating its northern promontory. The village retains in slightly modified form its old Greek name of Therapeia, meaning cure or healing. This name was given to the village in the early fifth century by the Patriarch Atticus, who wanted to disguise its ancient pagan name of Pharmakeus. This baleful name derived from the legend that Medea, in her pursuit of Jason, threw into the waters of the bay here the poison with which she intended to kill him.

Therapeia figured in the war fought between Venice and Genoa in the years 1350-55, in which the Byzantines sided with the Venetians. A major battle in this war was fought on 13 February 1352 at the mouth of the Bosphorus off Constantinople, in which

RUMELİHİSARI TO RUMELİKAVAĞI

Istenia, near Therapia

Therapia, and the Giant's Grave

both sides suffered great losses in men and ships, with neither the Genoese nor Venetians being able to claim a victory. After the battle the Genoese took refuge in their own harbor on the Golden Horn in Galata, while the Venetians, commanded by Admiral Nicolo Pisani, sailed up the Bosphorus and anchored in Therapeia. The Venetian fleet remained in Therapeia until April of that year, when Pisani sailed away with his remaining ships to return to Venice, leaving the Byzantines to fight alone against the Genoese. The Emperor, John VI Cantacuzenos (1347-54; co-emperor with John V Palaeologus,1341-91), had no choice but to make a treaty of his own with the Genoese, signed on 6 May 1352. This treaty renewed the commercial privileges of the Genoese in Constantinople and confirmed the independence of Galata, and it also gave Genoa control of a number of ports and fortresses in Byzantine territory, including the great castle of Yoros on the Asian shore of the upper Bosphorus.

Tarabya was particularly famous as a resort in the eighteenth and nineteenth centuries, when the Phanariotes, the Greek aristocracy of the Fener quarter of Stamboul, came here to spend the summer months. At the beginning of the nineteenth century the European powers began to build summer residences for their embassies along the Bosphorus around Tarabya, erecting them on land granted to them by the Sultans, with extensive gardens around the *yalı*s. The village was predominately Greek up until the mid-twentieth century, but now only a few Greek families remain. The dome of the Greek Orthodox church can be seen above an intervening building on the shore at the southern end of the village.

Evliya Çelebi has a different theory concerning the origin of Tarabya's name, which though apocryphal has some interesting bits of information and gives a picture of the village before it became a famous resort.

There stood here formerly a *dalyan* or fishgarth. Selim II, having taken delight in this place in catching fish, which were roasted under the shade of some tall cypress trees, commanded his Grand Vezir, Sokollu Mehmet Paşa, to erect on the spot a palace, which from the amusement (*tarab*)

RUMELİHİSARI TO RUMELİKAVAĞI 83

the Emperor enjoyed, was called Tarabya. This was its foundation. In the time of Sultan Murat I [1359-89], when the Russians invaded Yeniköy, the inhabitants of Tarabya gave battle to the Cossacks, and refused to give them the least thing, not even a grain of mustard. The Cossacks, enraged at this behavior, set fire to the place and burnt it down. It has since then been raised to its present state. There are eight hundred houses, one quarter of Muslims and a mosque, with seven quarters of Infidels. Where the *dalyan* and the cypress trees stood is now a shore-palace of the Inspector of Customs, and is the highest in the place. There is no bath and no kitchen for the poor, but there are forty small streets and many gardens.

The *dalyan* that Evliya mentions was one of many that existed in all of the bays of the Bosphorus up until quite recent times, with only one remaining now, at Beykoz on the Asian shore. It consists of a series of nets strung from piles driven into the shallow waters of the bay, and which are drawn up when a school of fish enters the enclosure.

Just beyond the Tarabya Hotel is the old French summer embassy. This late eighteenth-century *yalı* originally belonged to Prince Ypsilantis, a Phanariote Greek who was the Ottoman Hospodar, or Viceroy, of the trans-Danubian principalities of Moldavia and Wallachia. The *yalı* was presented to the French in 1807 by Selim III, who that same year was deposed by the Janissaries and then executed by them the following year. The building was badly damaged by fire in 1923, but it was rebuilt in the same style. Beyond that is the Italian summer consulate, rebuilt in 1906. The original Italian summer embassy here was a *yalı* presented by Abdülhamit II to Princess Elena, daughter of King Nicholas I of Montenegro, on the occasion of her marriage to King Victor Emmanuel III of Italy. Beyond that, on the outskirts of Tarabya, are the gardens of the old British summer embassy, which was destroyed by fire in 1911 and never rebuilt. The grounds are still used by the British Consulate.

Beyond Tarabya the European shore curves northwest and then due west to Kireçburnu, Lime Point, which looks northeastward directly toward the mouth of the Bosphorus on the Black Sea. This was known in Byzantine times as Kledai tou Pontou, the Keys of the Pontus, for here travelers going up the strait see the Black Sea for the first time. Today Kireçburnu is a tiny hamlet with a number of fish-restaurants.

Beyond Kireçburnu the shore continues northwestward as far as Kefeliköy and then bends sharply northeastward, thus forming Büyükdere Limanı, the deepest indentation on the strait, where the Bosphorus is some 3,500 meters wide. Then on the northern shore the ferry stops at the *iskele* in the village of Büyükdere, where the picturesque waterfront has now being somewhat spoiled by the new highway that runs in front of it.

The village takes its Turkish name from the great (*büyük*) valley (*dere*) at the head of the bay, a place known to the Byzantines as Kalos Agros, the Beautiful Meadow. The knights of the First Crusade camped here before they crossed the Bosphorus on their way into Asia Minor in 1096, and up until the late nineteenth century an ancient plane tree was pointed out as the place where Godefroy de Bouillon pitched his tent. Justinian founded a church here dedicated to St. Theodore of Tiron, and in the late eighth century the Patriarch Taraise founded a convent dedicated to All the Saints, where he was buried, and where a number of Byzantine empresses and princesses retired in their latter years. Evliya gives his customary description of the village as it was in his time:

This was also a pleasure-place of Sultans Selim I and II, who delighted in fishing here. It is surrounded by thick woods, which are impenetrable to the sun. In this great valley are cypresses, planes, weeping willows and other tall trees, the shade of which affords situations for garden sofas and prayer-places. The pleasure parties of Sultan Selim I were the origin of the village built near this valley. There are altogether a thousand small houses, one quarter of Muslims and seven of fishermen, boatmen and gardeners, all Infidels. By the landing-place is a mosque, built by Koca Defterdar Paşa, a bath, and some small streets, with a number of gardens.

The infidels of whom Evliya speaks were mostly Greeks, with some Armenians, both communities now being much smaller than they were in times past. Nevertheless, there are still two churches in Büyükdere, one Greek Orthodox and the other Armenian Catholic.

The most notable mosque is in Çayırbaşı, at the head of the bay south of the village. This is Kaptan-ı Derya Cezayirli Gazi Hasan Paşa Camii, built in the late eighteenth century. The founder was the famous Cezayirli (the Algerian) Gazi (Warrior for the Faith) Hasan Paşa, High Admiral of the Ottoman Navy in the reign of Abdülhamit I, and also the Sultan's son-in-law. Hasan Paşa, who was also known as Cezayirli Palabıyık, the "scimitar-mustached Algerian," left his native Algeria at the age of fourteen and went to sea, jumping ship at Gallipoli in the Dardanelles, where he worked for a while in a coffee house before joining the Ottoman Navy as a cabin boy. He worked his way up through the ranks and eventually was given command of a warship. He was the only Turk to emerge as a hero from the battle of Çeşme on 5 July 1770, when the Russians trapped the Ottoman fleet in the harbor and virtually annihilated it. Hasan Paşa's ship was badly damaged, but he managed to sail it through the surrounding Russian fleet and made it as far as Ayvalık before it sank, after which he led his crew overland to Istanbul. He then persuaded the Sultan to let him build a new fleet to do battle with the Russians, who were besieging the Ottoman fortress on the Aegean island of Lemnos. The Sultan agreed, and the following year Hasan Paşa set off from Istanbul in his new fleet, which he had manned with the riff-raff of Galata, including all the able-bodied galley slaves in the prison. As he sailed off one vezir was heard to remark: "We have nothing to lose, for if Hasan Paşa wins we retain Lemnos, and if he loses we are rid of all the scum of Galata!" Hasan Paşa emerged victorious, defeating the Russians and breaking their siege of Lemnos, after which he returned in triumph to Istanbul. The Sultan rewarded Hasan Paşa by making him commanding admiral of the Ottoman fleet and giving him the hand of his daughter in marriage, after which he built this mosque in Büyükdere. There is a fine bronze statue of Hasan Paşa by the Naval Headquarters at Kasım Paşa on the Golden Horn, showing him with the pet panther with which he strolled along the quay in Galata in his latter years, terrifying all who passed.

In the fields around Hasan Paşa's mosque there is a large Gypsy encampment. This has grown larger in recent years since the demolition of the ancient Gypsy village in Sulukule, on the Sixth Hill of the old city just inside the Theodosian walls, where they had been living since the fourteenth century.

There are also two old summer embassies in Büyükdere, the Spanish and the Russian. Next to the former is the Spanish Chapel, a handsome neo-Gothic edifice that still serves as a Roman Catholic church.

One of the grandest of the mansions along the shore in the northern outskirts of Büyükdere is the Azaryan Yalısı. This was built in the late nineteenth century by an Armenian named Manuk Azaryan Efendi, who served in both the Parliament and the foreign service during the last years of the Ottoman Empire. Today the *yalı* houses the Sadberk Hanım Museum, a unique and rich collection of antiquities and Turkish works of art, which opened on 14 October 1980. The museum is dedicated to the memory of Sadberk Hanım, late wife of Vehbi Koç, one of Turkey's leading businessmen. Originally the objects on display in the museum were from Sadberk Koç's personal collection of antiques that she had built up over a lifetime. Through a donation made by the Koç family in 1983, a decade after her death, the museum acquired a distinguished collection of antiquities that had been put together by the world-famous Turkish collector Hüseyin Kocabaş.

The museum is divided into two wings, the Turkish-Islamic Art Section and the Archaeological Section. In the first of these two sections, the exhibits on the ground floor begin with metal objects of the Early Islamic period (ninth-tenth centuries). These

Büyükdere: Saberk Hanım Müzesi

are followed by works in tombak and metal objects from Ottoman times. The displays continue with a collection of silver bearing the imperial monograms (*tuğra*) of the Ottoman sultans, jewel-encrusted timepieces, jewelry, celadon ware, blue-and-white and polychrome Chinese porcelains, and examples of İznik, Kütahya, and Çanakkale tiles and pottery beginning with the fifteenth century. On the upper floor are life-sized dioramas that show details of traditional Turkish customs and ways of life, a postpartum confinement room, a bridal shower, and a circumcision bed. There are also exquisite examples of Turkish embroideries on display, as well as costumes of the late Ottoman period. The displays in the Archaeological Section are arranged in chronological order beginning with the Late Neolithic-Early Chalcolithic (6000 BC), Early Bronze (3000 BC), the Assyrian Trade Colonies and Hittites (2000 BC), and the Urartian and Phrygian civilizations (1000 BC), continuing on with examples of the Mycenaean, Geometric, Orientalizing, Archaic, Classical, Hellenistic and Roman periods, culminating with works of the Byzantine era. Among the works on display are terracotta figurines, pottery and ceramics, jewelry, inscribed tablets, glass and crystal objects, ivories, and objects made from bronze, silver, gold and electrum, including coins. The two sections together represent a truc muscum of Anatolian civilizations.

A road leads from Çayırbaşı inland through the great valley of Büyükdere. At the inner end of the valley it passes through the Belgrade Forest, the largest tract of woodland on the European shore of the Bosphorus. The forest takes its name from the village of Belgrade that once stood in its midst. The village was founded in 1521 by Süleyman the Magnificent after his conquest of the city of Belgrade, when he transported a certain number of the inhabitants of that city and settled them here in order to look after the reservoirs and other waterworks with which the forest abounds. Beginning in the seventeenth century the European powers who were represented at the Sublime Porte built summer embassies in and around the village of Belgrade. Lady Mary Wortley Montagu describes the village in some of her famous letters, written when

RUMELİHİSARI TO RUMELİKAVAĞI 89

her husband, Sir Edward Montagu, was English ambassador in Istanbul in the years 1716-18. The summer embassies were moved to Tarabya in the nineteenth century, after which the village of Belgrade declined, to be abandoned altogether in 1898, when the government moved its inhabitants elsewhere. Virtually nothing now remains of the village except the foundations of a few of its houses. The Belgrade Forest itself suffered severe damage in 1826, when the New Army of Mahmut II set the woods afire to smoke out the Janissaries who had taken refuge there after the main body of their corps had been virtually annihilated by the Sultan's troops in Istanbul.

There are numerous impressive aqueducts and reservoirs scattered throughout the countryside from the Belgrade Forest to the upper reaches of the streams that feed the Golden Horn. Most of the aqueducts were built by Sinan for Süleyman the Magnificent, some of them undoubtedly replacing Byzantine structures dating back to the time of Justinian. The first aqueduct one comes to, not far up the valley of Büyükdere, is later commissioned by Mahmut I and completed in 1732, conveying water from the Sultan's reservoir and several others to the *taksim*, or water distribution center, that he built in what is now Taksim Square in Istanbul. Mahmut's reservoir (in Turkish, *bend*) is a magnificent structure, with its great dam built of Proconnesian marble. The two aqueducts of Sinan that are the most easily accessible because they are on the main road are also the longest and most impressive. Both are near the village of Burgaz, the ancient Pyrgos. The first, which is 342 meters long, is called Eğrikemer, the Bent Aqueduct, because it consists of two segments that meet in an obtuse angle. This aqueduct seems to have been built originally by Andronicus I Comnenus (1183-85); it was in ruins when Gyllius saw it, and Sinan must have rebuilt it almost completely, for all the visible masonry appears to be of his time. Sinan's other nearby work, Uzunkemer, the Long Aqueduct, is beyond Burgaz; it is 716 meters in length and strides across the valley in a most Roman manner. These two aqueducts span the valley of the Barbyzes, the stream now called

90 *RUMELİHİSARI TO RUMELİKAVAĞI*

Kâğıthane Suyu, which flows into the Golden Horn. This stream and its twin, the Alibey Suyu, the ancient Cidaris, together form the once famous Sweet Waters of Europe, which in the eighteenth century was a favorite resort of Ottoman society. The Alibey Suyu is also spanned by two aqueducts of Sinan; these are much harder to find because the road is quite bad; they are also much smaller but at the same time more picturesque because closely hemmed in by high hills. The one across the Alibey Suyu itself is called Maglova Kemeri, though in English it is known as Justinian's Aqueduct; Gyllius saw this too in ruins, but it was entirely rebuilt by Sinan. The other, which spans a tributary of the Alibey Suyu, is appropriately called Güzelce Kemer, the Charming Aqueduct, for it is indeed very pretty. All four of these aqueducts, together with several smaller ones, conduct the water from various reservoirs scattered throughout the countryside and convey it to the *taksim* at Eğrikapı on the Sixth Hill, from where it is distributed throughout Stamboul. Sinan was working on this elaborate system of aqueducts during the decade 1554-64.

After leaving Büyükdere the ferry rounds Mesar Burnu, the Cape of Joy, where there is a castle-like edifice in neo-Gothic style that now serves as a Turkish Naval Officers' Club. In antiquity this cape was known as the Promontorium Simas, where in the seventh century BC the Megarians raised a monument that was for long a landmark for mariners en route to the Euxine.

The ferry stops next at the *iskele* in Sarıyer, the largest village on the European shore of the upper Bosphorus and the most important fishing port on the strait. The fishing boats of Sarıyer range from the Black Sea through the Bosphorus, the Sea of Marmara, the Dardanelles, and on into the Aegean, disgorging their catch at the very colorful fish market in the port, where there are several quay-side restaurants. This is the liveliest village on the Bosphorus, inhabited principally by fishermen and their families, though in recent years a number of wealthy Iranian and Arab emigres have taken up residence here.

From Sarıyer a road leads inland and after a drive of some 15

RUMELİHİSARI TO RUMELİKAVAĞI 91

kilometers brings us to Kilyos on the Black Sea. The first part of this drive passes lookout points where we command magnificent views of the upper Bosphorus, and one or two from which we can see almost the whole length of the strait from the Black Sea to the Sea of Marmara. Approaching Kilyos there is a good view of the Black Sea and the long sandy beach that extends for miles along the Thracian coast. As the road starts downhill we can see off in the distance an ancient pyrgos, or watchtower, known as Ovid's Tower. The name comes from a fanciful association of the tower with the Roman poet Ovid, who in AD 8 passed through the Bosphorus on his way to exile on the coast of the Euxine at Tomi, now the Bulgarian city of Varna, where he died ten years later. The tower has never been studied by archaeologists, but from its appearance it would seem to be a pyrgos of the Hellenistic period, one of many that can still be seen on the Aegean isles of Greece. At the final approach to Kilyos we see on the left three large ruined towers; these are known in Turkish as *suterazisi*, and were water-control towers for the aqueduct that once brought water to the village. The village itself perches on a promontory above the sea; at the highest point there are the substantial ruins of a fourteenth-century Genoese fortress, but this is in a military zone and thus off-limits to the public.

After leaving Sarıyer the ferry passes Yenimahalle, the New Quarter, which as its name implies is a new suburb of Sarıyer. Beyond Yenimahalle we pass a number of small boatyards along the shore, where many of the wooden fishing boats of the Bosphorus are still built and repaired by local shipwrights. We then come to Tellibaba Burnu, the promontory where ships entering the Bosphorus can pick up a pilot to steer them down the strait. The promontory takes its name from Telli Baba, a famous Muslim saint who is buried in a *türbe* on the hilltop above. This is one of the most popular Muslim shrines in Istanbul, particularly among young women, who come here to pray to Telli Baba to find them a good husband. Those who are successful, and they seem to include most of the brides in Istanbul, come here on their

RUMELİHİSARI TO RUMELİKAVAĞI

wedding day with their grooms in tow, and after saying a prayer of thanks to Telli Baba they attach strands of gold wire to the grating around his tomb as talismans. Telli Baba, whose name means literally the "Wired-up Saint," is said to be in mystic communication with the Prophet Joshua, in Turkish Yuşa, whose supposed tomb is on the hilltop due south across the strait.

After rounding Tellibaba Burnu the ferry comes to the *iskele* at Rumelikavağı, the last stop on the European shore of the Bosphorus.

CHAPTER SIX
THE UPPER BOSPHORUS

The upper Bosphorus can be said to begin at Rumelikavağı and Anadolukavağı, the European and Asian Poplars, for they are the last ferry stops on either side of the strait. There is no shore road up either side of the Bosphorus beyond the northern environs of these two villages, and so those who want to go up to the mouth of the strait on the Black Sea must do so by private boat, or by making an arrangement with a boatman at one of the fishing villages on the upper Bosphorus.

An excursion by boat along the shores of the upper Bosphorus can be one of great delight, for both shores are wild, rugged and desolate, but extremely beautiful. Now for the first time on the strait one finds sandy beaches hidden away in secluded coves; grey herons haunt the cliffs; black cormorants dive into the limpid water; great clouds of shearwaters, those "lost souls" of the Bosphorus, skim the surface of the sea; and schools of dolphins often gambol by. Many features of the upper Bosphorus have associations with the epic voyage of Jason and the Argonauts, and these have been identified by Gyllius in his pioneering work on the strait, adding further interest to this excursion.

Rumelikavağı consists of a small cluster of houses around the *iskele*, on either side of which there are a number of fish restaurants. The view from the *iskele* is superb, including the whole of the upper Bosphorus out to the Black Sea. On the Asian shore directly opposite we see the ruins of the great fortress of Yoros, which, together with a castle on the European side, made up the principal Byzantine defences and customs-control points on the upper Bosphorus. Only a few scattered ruins remain of the European castle; these are on the hill above Rumelikavağı and are known locally as Karataş, or Black Stone. The ruined batteries below the castles on either side are relatively modern Turkish works; they were built in 1783 by Toussaint and strengthened in 1794 by Monnier, two French military engineers in the Ottoman service.

The villages of Rumelikavağı and Anadolukavağı are probably to be identified with the ancient Serapion and Hieron, respectively. These were the Byzantine toll and customs control points, and a chain was stretched between them on buoys to prevent ships from passing through the strait without paying their fees. (A similar chain was stretched across the Bosphorus by the Turkish Navy up until the early 1960s, and from it there was suspended a net to prevent the passage of Russian submarines.). Both of these posts were guarded by fortresses on the hills above. The fortress on the European side was built by Manuel I Comnenus (1143-80) and called the Castle of the Incorporeal Saints; the one on the Asian side, founded at some time during the dynasty of the Palaeologues, who ruled Byzantium in the period 1261-1453, was called the Castle of Hieron. The Genoese took control of both fortresses in 1352, according to the peace treaty they signed with John VI Cantacuzenos on 6 May of that year, after which they collected the tolls and customs fees from shipping in the Bosphorus, further contributing to the decline of the Byzantine Empire. Mehmet II captured both fortresses in 1452, and after the Turkish Conquest they were abandoned and eventually fell into ruins.

In antiquity two temples stood on the site of these castles, the one on the European side erected by the people of Byzantium and the Asian by those of Chalcedon. The temple on the European side was dedicated to Cybele, the fertility goddess of Phrygia in Asia Minor, and the one in Asia to the Twelve Olympian Gods. The first sanctuaries on these sites, according to mythology, had been altars erected by Jason in thanksgiving after his return from the land of Colchis with the Golden Fleece. In Byzantine times there was a convent on the European side known as the Mavromoliotissa, founded by the Empress Eudoxia, wife of Romanus IV Diogenes (1067-81). The convent was demolished in 1713 because it was in a military zone.

Beyond Rumelikavağı the shore road continues for some 300

Fort Biel-Gorod

The Bosphorus opposite the Genoese Castle

meters to Altınkum, or Golden Sands, the first of the sandy beaches, shaded by a pleasant grove of acacia trees. For the next 2.5 kilometers beyond Altınkum the shore rises up in precipitous cliffs sparsely covered with shrubs, a stretch that shows no sign of ever having been inhabited. We then come to a wide but shallow bay known as Büyükliman, the Great Harbor; in antiquity this was called, for reasons unknown, the Harbor of the Ephesians. On the shore there are the ruins of a number of buildings, including a *hamam*; the beach is sandy and the valley behind it is wooded and attractive, making this a pleasant place to swim or picnic.

Another kilometer or so farther along we come to an oddly shaped and very craggy promontory known as Garipçe Burnu, or the Strange Cape, an appropriate name. There is a fairly well preserved Ottoman fortress here; this was built in 1773 for Mustafa III by the Baron de Tott, another French military engineer in the Turkish service.

The ancient name of this place, according to Gyllius, was Gyropolis, the Place of Vultures. It received its name through the myth of King Phineus, the blind old prophet who was the son-in-law of Boreas, god of the North Wind. It seems that Phineus was tormented by the Harpies, winged female monsters who, every time a meal was set before the King, would swoop down upon the food and snatch most of it away, leaving the remainder with such a loathsome stench that it was inedible. As a result, Phineus had almost wasted away by the time that Jason and the Argonauts arrived on their journey up the Bosphorus in quest of the Golden Fleece. Among them were Zetes and Calais, the winged sons of Boreas, who took pity on King Phineus, their brother-in-law, whereupon they flew up and chased away the Harpies, who never returned. In return the grateful Phineus advised the Argonauts about the rest of their journey, particularly on how to make their way safely past the dreaded Symplegades, the Clashing Rocks at the mouth of the Bosphorus, also known as the Cyanean Rocks because of their blue color. As Apollonius of Rhodes quotes King Phineus in his *Argonautica*:

THE UPPER BOSPHORUS

When you leave me, the first thing you will see will be the two Cyanean Rocks, at the end of the strait. To the best of my knowledge, no one has ever made his way between them, for not being fixed to the bottom of the sea they frequently collide, flinging up the water in a seething mass which falls on the rocky flanks of the straits with a resounding roar. Now as I take it you are god-fearing travelers and men of sense, you will be advised by me: you will not rashly throw away your lives or rush into danger with the recklessness of youth. Make an experiment first. Send out a dove from Argo to explore the way. If she succeeds in flying between the Rocks and out across the sea, do not hesitate to follow in her path, but get a firm grip on your oars and cleave the water of the strait. For that is the time when salvation will depend, not on your prayers, but on your strength of arm. So think of nothing else, be firm, and spend your energies on what will pay you best. By all means pray to the gods, but choose an earlier moment. And if the dove flies on, but comes to grief midway, turn back. It is always better to submit to Heaven; and you could not possibly escape a dreadful end. The Rocks would crush you, even if Argo were an iron ship. Ah, my poor friends, I do implore you not to disregard my counsel from the gods, even if you imagine their hatred of myself to be far more bitter than in fact it is. Do not dare to sail farther in, if the bird's failure warns you to desist.

The Argonauts were dismayed when they heard this, but they agreed to take his advice when they reached the Clashing Rocks, as we will see when we come upon them ourselves, 2.3 kilometers due north of Garipçe Burnu.

Gyllius identified two sets of Cyanean rocks, one on either side of the Bosphorus at its mouth on the Black Sea, with the group on the European side more obviously matching the description in the *Argonautica*. The European group, which in Turkish is known as İreke Taşı, or Midwife's Stool, is a striking feature at the very mouth of the Bosphorus, some 100 meters offshore from Rumelifeneri, the Lighthouse of Europe. There is a tiny fishing village on the headland and the remains of an Ottoman fort built in 1769 by a Greek military engineer in the Turkish service. The huge rock, which is now joined to the shore by a concrete mole, is about twenty meters high and about 200 meters in circumference, divided by deep fissures into several parts. On the highest plateau of the rock there are the remains of a monument known as the Column of Pompey. "The ascent to this peak," says Gyllius, "is not open except by one approach, and this, extremely narrow, so that one must climb up on all fours." Nowadays there are two approaches, one slightly easier than the other, but both disagreeable enough for one who is terrified of heights. The reward of intrepidity is a fine view of the Black Sea and the mouth of the Bosphorus, and the base of Pompey's Column. This is not really a column base but an ancient altar, decorated with a garlanded ram's head and other reliefs now much worn; it has traces of a Latin inscription, now no longer legible, the transcription and interpretation of which is debated. Certainly neither altar nor column had anything to do with Pompey, and it is not known who first gave it this misleading name; it was after the time of Gyllius, however, since he does not mention it. Gyllius thought that the altar was probably the remnant of a shrine to Apollo, which Dionysius Byzantius says the Romans erected on one of the Cyanean Rocks. The column itself, with its Corinthian capital, toppled down during a storm in April 1680 and had utterly disappeared by 1800.

On a stormy day the huge waves rolling in from the Black Sea smash through the fissures in the Symplegades in great clouds of foaming spray, making it appear as if the rocks are indeed thunderously clashing together, at least if you use your imagination. Then is the time to read the climactic passage in the *Argonautica*, where Apollonius describes how the steersman Tiphys managed to get Argo through, heeding the advice they had been given by King Phineus, and with a little help at the right moment from the goddess Athena, who had been watching over them:

In due course they found themselves entering the narrowest part of the winding strait. Rugged cliffs hemmed them in on either side, and Argo as she advanced began to feel a swirling undercurrent. They moved ahead in

THE UPPER BOSPHORUS 99

fear, for now the clash of the colliding Rocks and the thunder of surf on the shores fell ceaselessly on their ears. Euphemus seized the dove and climbed on the prow, while the oarsmen, at Tiphys' orders, made a special effort, hoping by their own strength of arm to drive Argo through the Rocks forthwith. They rounded a bend and saw a thing that no one after them has seen - the Rocks were moving apart. Their hearts sank; but now Euphemus launched the dove on her flight and the eyes of all were raised to watch her as she passed between the Rocks.

Once more the Rocks met face to face with a resounding crash, flinging a great cloud of spray into the air. The sea gave a terrific roar and the broad sky rang again. Caverns underneath the crags bellowed as the sea came surging in. A great wave broke through the cliff and thefoam swept high above them. Argo was swung around as the flood reached her.

But the dove got through, unscathed but for the tips of her tail-feathers, which were nipped off by the Rocks. The oarsmen gave a shout of triumph and Tiphys shouted at them to row with all their might, for the Rocks were opening again. So they rowed on full of dread, till the backwash, overtaking them, thrust Argo in between the Rocks. Then the fears of all were turned to panic. Sheer destruction hung above their heads.

They had already reached a point where they could see the vast sea opening out on either side, when they were suddenly faced by a tremendous billow arched like an overhanging rock. They bent their heads down at the sight, for it seemed about to fall and overwhelm the ship. But Tiphys just in time checked her as she plunged forward and the great wave slid under her keel. Indeed it raised her stern so high in the air that she was carried clear of the Rocks. Euphemus ran along shouting to all his friends to put their backs into their rowing, and with answering shouts they struck the water. Yet for every foot that Argo made she lost two, though the oars bent like curved bows as the men put out their strength.

But now another overwhelming wave came rushing down on them, and when Argo had shot end-on like a rolling-pin through the hollow lap of this terrific sea, she found herself held back by the swirling tide just in the place where the Rocks met. To left and right they shook and rumbled; but Argo could not budge.

This was the moment when Athena intervened. Holding on to the hard rock with her left hand, she pushed the ship through with the other; and Argo clove the air like a winged arrow, though even so the Rocks, clashing in their accustomed way, sheared off the tip of the mascot on the stern. When the men had thus got through unhurt, Athena soared up to Olympus. But the rocks were now rooted forever in one spot close to one another. It had been decided by the happy gods that this should be their fate when a human being had seen them and sailed through. The Argonauts, freed from the cold grip of panic, breathed again when they saw the sky once more and the vast ocean stretching out ahead. They felt that they had come through Hell alive.

We now cross the mouth of the Bosphorus from Rumelifeneri to Anadolufeneri, the Lighthouse of Asia, with the limitless sea stretching off to the horizon in the north and in the south the verdant hills of Europe and Asia cleaving apart to reveal the strait, down which we can see for some six miles as far as Kledai tou Pontou, the Keys of the Pontus.

Anadolufeneri is a small village perched on the hill above the promontory that marks the mouth of the Bosphorus on the Asian side, with the lighthouse itself on the brow of the hill. There have been lighthouses here and at Rumelifeneri since antiquity, guiding mariners on their way into the strait, whose entrance is difficult to discern even in broad daylight. As Evliya Çelebi writes of Anadolufeneri. "On the top of a high tower is a great beacon lighted with whale oil, by which ships sailing on the Black Sea find their way into the Canal."

As we approach Anadolufeneri we have a long view down the Anatolia coast beyond the mouth of the Bosphorus, first the bay known as Kabakoz Limanı and then the promontory called Yum Burnu, then beyond that another indentation where the river known as Riva Deresi enters the Black Sea, and beyond that another cape and the islet called Eşek Adası. These are features mentioned by King Phineus in his directions for the Argonauts once they made their way past the Clashing Rocks, though in all but one case their

THE UPPER BOSPHORUS 101

names have changed:

Well, all this will happen as it must. But if you come safely through the Clashing Rocks into the Euxine, sail on with the land of the Bithynians on your right, shunning the coastal reef, till you round the mouth of the swift River Rhebas and the Black Cape and come to harbor in the Isle of Thynias.

The Asian shore of the upper Bosphorus is very imperfectly known, and seems to have been rarely visited even by the few travellers who write about it. The only reliable guide is Gyllius, for he alone appears to have explored the region in detail. Even Gyllius' account, however, is not free of difficulty, for he never gives the Turkish names of places in this region, perhaps because in his time they didn't yet have any. Nevertheless, there are four places in his narrative that can be identified with certainty: the River Rhebas, the Promontorium Ancyraeum, the Promontorium Coracium, and the Fanum Jovis; and from these the others can be worked out. The Rhebas still retains a version of its ancient name: Riva Deresi; it is a river that flows into the Black Sea about four kilometers beyond the mouth of the Bosphorus, and just beyond it is the great table-like rocky offshore islet that he calls Colonean but which is now known as Eşek Adası, Donkey Island. Riva is very attractive and picturesque with its fourteenth-century castle at the end of a long sandy beach, a fine place to swim and picnic.

The Promontorium Ancyraeum is Yum Burnu, Cape of Good Omen, which is just at the mouth of the Bosphorus. The ancient name means the Cape of the Anchor, stemming from the legend that it was here that Jason took on a stone anchor for Argo. In Gyllius' time it was known to the local Greeks as Akri Psomion, or Cape Bread, perhaps because of its supposed resemblance to the rock-like bread that the Greeks call *paximadhi*, which is often used as a place name for rocky headlands or offshore islets. The reef that has the best claim to be the Asian Cyanean Rock stands under the southern cliff face of Yum Burnu and is thus described

THE UPPER BOSPHORUS

by Gyllius, a description which is perfectly applicable to this day:

The reef is divided into four rocks above water which, however, are joined below; it is separated from the continent by a narrow channel filled with many stones, by which as by a staircase one can cross the channel with dry feet when the sea is calm; but when the sea is rough waves surround the four rocks into which I said the reef is divided. Three of these are low and more or less submerged, but the middle one is higher than the European rock, sloping up to an acute point and roundish at the summit; it is splashed by the waves but not submerged, and is everywhere precipitous and straight.

The bay to the south of Yum Burnu is now called Kabakoz Limanı, the Harbor of the Wild Walnuts; in Gyllius' time it was known among the local Greeks as Ayios Sideros. On the south this bay is bounded by a point not named by Gyllius but nowadays called Anadolufeneri Burnu, after the lighthouse on the promontory, with the village of the same name on the heights above. Just south of this is the bay which Gyllius called Ampelodes, now Çakal Limanı, the Harbor of Jackals, fringed by savage and rocky precipices. The next promontory beyond this, unnamed by Gyllius, is now called Poyraz Burnu. (In Turkish Poyraz is the fierce northeast wind that howls down the Bosphorus in winter; its name is a corruption of Boreas, the Greek god of the north wind.). On Poyraz Burnu, just opposite Garipçe and like it strangely shaped, is a craggy headland surmounted by an Ottoman fortress built in 1773 by the Baron de Tott, and another small village. The long sandy beach to the south is now known as Poyraz Bay; the Greeks of Gyllius time called it Dios Sacra, as he writes: "because, I suppose, there was once an altar here either of Jove or of Neptune, the other Jove." This is one of the most pleasant places on the Bosphorus to swim and spend a leisurely afternoon. The bay is bounded on the south by Fil Burnu, Elephant Point; in Gyllius' time it was called Coracium, or Rooky, "because the Greeks of this age say that ravens are wont to build their nests there." The

Rumelifeneri: Harbor of the "Clashing Rocks"

Genoese Castle above Anadolukavağı

long stretch of coast between here and Anadolukavağı is hardly to be described as a bay, so rugged and precipitous is it. It is now called Keçili Liman, Goats' Harbor, and we have seen not only goats and sheep but even cows grazing on its rather barren slopes.

We now pass in succession three small bays: Keçilik, Tahaffuzhane and Hacıağzı, all three of which are good anchorages where one can stop for a swim. Tahaffuzhane means "Quarantine Station," which is what the buildings there were used for up until late Ottoman times.

We now pass under the great Castle of Yoros, also known as the Genoese Castle, which we will visit from Anadolukavağı, which comes into view as we round the promontory at Kavak Burnu, Poplar Point, where the Turkish Navy has a communications and navigation station. As we pass the naval base, we see within its grounds by the shore a late Ottoman mansion known as the House of Marco Paşa. Marco Paşa was an Istanbul Greek who became a distinguished physician and rose to high rank in the Ottoman service, renowned for his ability to solve problems of all types. In his day if anyone in Istanbul had a problem they went to see Marco Paşa, and invariably he solved it. His name is perpetuated in an Istanbul proverb, for if anyone complains about their problems the cynical response is "Go tell it to Marco Paşa."

After passing the naval base we come to the *iskele* at Anadolukavağı, where our exploration of the upper Bosphorus comes to an end.

CHAPTER SEVEN
ANADOLUKAVAĞI
TO ANADOLUHİSARI

Anadolukavağı, the Anatolian Poplar, is the last stop on the Asian shore for ferries going up the Bosphorus. The fortifications here, like those at Rumelikavağı, were built in 1783 by Toussaint and strengthened in 1794 by Monnier. There are a number of fish restaurants around the *iskele* where one can have lunch after exploring the upper Bosphorus, and before going on to look at the great fortress north of the village. A road leads from the village and goes around the inner periphery of the fortress to its highest point, on Yoros Tepesi. From there one can walk down through the various levels of the fortress and regain the road lower down the hill, from where one can stroll back to the village.

Yoros Tepesi was identified by Gyllius as the Fane of Jove, by which he means the temple of Zeus Ourious, Zeus of the Favoring Wind, and the Hieron, or sacred precinct, where there were shrines of the Twelve Olympian Gods. He was led to this identification by the name Yoros, doubtless a corruption of Ourious. According to one version of the myth, the temple or temples were founded by Phrixos, son of King Athamas of Boeotia and Nephele, goddess of the clouds. Athamas was about to sacrifice Phrixos and his sister Helle during a time of drought, but Nephele saved her children by sending them off to the land of Colchis on a flying ram with golden fleece that had been given to her by Hermes. When they passed over the first of the two straits separating Europe from Asia, Helle fell off the ram and was drowned, and thenceforth the strait was called the Hellespont in her memory. Phrixos stopped here on the Asian shore of the upper Bosphorus to dedicate a sanctuary to the Twelve Olympian Gods, after which he flew off on the flying ram to Colchis, where he was received with honors by King Areetes. As a token of gratitude for his safe arrival there Phrixos sacrificed the ram to Zeus; he then gave the golden fleece to Areetes, who hung it in a grove of trees sacred to Ares. This was the famous golden fleece that led Jason to embark on his epic voyage, and after he succeeded in taking it from Colchis with the aid of Medea, the King's daughter, he set out on his return voyage. In another version of the myth the sanctuary of Zeus Ourious here was founded by Jason on his return voyage. Whoever the founder, this was undoubtedly the temple that Herodotus mentions in connection with the bridge built across the Bosphorus in 512 BC, when King Darius sailed up the strait to visit the sanctuary here and view the Euxine. In antiquity it was customary for mariners to make a sacrifice here to Zeus of the Favorable Wind before embarking on a voyage in the Euxine. Cicero mentions that there was a statue of Zeus Ourious here. The sanctuary was destroyed early in the Byzantine era, after which Justinian built a church dedicated to the Archangel Michael. Archaeological excavations on the hilltop in 1924 unearthed the foundations of Justinian's church as well as fragments of sculpture dating from the fifth century BC.

Anadolukavağı is on the site of ancient Hieron, the toll and customs control point on the Asian shore of the upper Bosphorus, protected by the fortress on what is now known as Yoros Tepesi. Hieron and the post of Serapion on the European shore opposite were the sites of frequent struggles for control of the strait. King Prusias of Bithynia captured Hieron from Byzantium in 192 BC, but soon afterwards he was forced to give it up. The two posts fell to the Romans in AD 196 when the Emperor Septimius Severus captured Byzantium. The Russians took Hieron and destroyed the fortress there when they raided down the Bosphorus in 942. The present fortress was probably built by the Palaeologues in the late thirteenth century, but in 1352 they were forced to turn it over to the Genoese, who appear to have rebuilt it thoroughly. Gyllius rather oddly describes this castle as small, though it is in fact by far the largest fortress on the Bosphorus, enclosing almost twice the area of Rumelihisarı; doubtless he was thinking not of the long surrounding walls but only of the citadel itself, probably the only part still garrisoned in his day. Evliya tells us that Beyazit I (1389-1403) built a mosque here and that Mehmet II restored and garrisoned the fortress.

At the lower end of the fortress there is a ramshackle café run by a local farmer, a delightful place from which one commands a sweeping view of the upper Bosphorus and its mouth on the Black Sea.

From Anadolukavağı one can also make an excursion to the peak of Yuşa Tepesi, which is due south of the village, approached by Yuşa Tepesi Yolu. Yuşa Tepesi, the Mount of Joshua, is the highest peak along the upper Bosphorus, with its summit 202 meters above sea level. The peak was known in antiquity as the Bed of Hercules, but from late Ottoman times onwards Western travellers have called it the Giant's Grave. The giant in question is a Muslim saint named Yuşa, whom some pious Turks believe to be the Prophet Joshua; his supposed grave is some twelve meters long, marked by green-painted stele at his head and feet. The saint's grave has now become a very popular place of pilgrimage, with a mosque erected next to the walled enclosure in which he is buried. The view from the summit is superb, with all of the upper Bosphorus in sight and a large part of the central course of the strait as well. Byron came here for the view during his visit to Istanbul in the spring of 1810, describing the scene in a memorable canto in *Don Juan:*

> The wind swept down the Euxine, and the wave
> Broke foaming o'er the blue Symplegades,
> 'Tis a grand sight from off the Giant's Grave
> To watch the progress of these rolling seas
> Between the Bosphorus, as they lash and lave
> Europe and Asia, you being quite at ease:
> There's not a sea the passenger e'er pukes in,
> Turns up more dangerous breakers than the Euxine.

108 ANADOLUKAVAĞI TO ANADOLUHİSARI

We now return to Anadolukavağı to board the ferry at the *iskele* there. The ferry takes us across Macar Bay and then around Acar Burnu, the promontory below Yuşa Tepesi. We then pass the Umar sand banks, two shallows marked by buoys off a precipitous and inhospitable coastline, after which we round Selvi Burnu and pass the village of Yalıköy, as the coast turns east to the charming valley of the Tokat Deresi. Here Mehmet the Conqueror built a royal kiosk, as did Süleyman the Magnificent. Gyllius described the latter building as a "royal villa shaded by woods of various trees, especially planes;" he goes on to mention the landing steps "by which the King, crossing the shallow shore of the sea, disembarks into his gardens." It is from these steps that the place gets its modern name, Hünkâr İskelesi, the Emperor's Landing Place, which in turn gave its name to the famous treaty of alliance that was signed here in 1833 by Prince Orloff of Russia and the Sublime Porte. Two years earlier Mehmet Ali, the Ottoman viceroy in Egypt, had sent an invading army under the command of his son İbrahim Paşa, who had swept through Syria and penetrated into Anatolia as far as Kütahya, threatening to attack Istanbul. Mahmut II accepted an offer of help from the Czar, who sent an army under Prince Orloff to defend Istanbul against İbrahim Paşa. The Russians landed at Hünkâr İskelesi and encamped in Tokat Deresi, remaining there until İbrahim Paşa was forced to withdraw to Syria. It was then that the Treaty of Hünkâr İskelesi was drawn up and signed, with the Sultan agreeing to consult the Czar on all matters affecting "tranquility and safety." The present palace of Hünkâr İskelesi, which we see in the center of a lovely grove of plane trees that obscure its lower floors, was built in the mid-nineteenth century by Sarkis Balyan for Sultan Abdülmecit. The palace is now a children's hospital.

The ferry now stops at the *iskele* in Beykoz, or Prince's Walnut, the largest village on the Asian shore of the upper Bosphorus. Beykoz, in addition to several large and handsome Ottoman houses in beautiful gardens, has an extraordinary street-fountain in the main village square. The Ottoman scholar Hafız Hüseyin Ayvansarayi, writing c. 1780 in his *Hadikat-il Cevami,* or Gardens of the Mosques, says of the Beykoz Çeşmesi that "This fountain has not its equal in beauty in all the villages of the Bosphorus." The *çeşme* forms a domed and columned loggia, very pretty indeed, and quite unlike any other Bosphorus fountain; its inscription dates it to 1746, and the Hadikat says it was commissioned by one İshak Ağa, Inspector of the Customs.

Gyllius is at pains to show that Beykoz was the home of the terrible Amycus, king of the savage Bebryces, whom Apollonius introduces at the beginning of Book II of the *Argonautica,* where the Argonauts land their ship in a wide bay on the Asian shore of the Bosphorus:

This was where Amycus, the arrogant king of the Bebyrces, had his farm and cattle yards. Born to Poseidon by the Bithynian nymph Melie, he was the world's greatest bully. It was his barbarous custom to allow no one, not even a foreign visitor, to leave his country before trying conclusions with him in a boxing-match. He had already killed a number of his neighbors. And now he came down to the ship, planted himself among the Argonauts and not even troubling to ask who they were or what had brought them overseas, had the effrontery to say:

'Listen, sailormen, to something you should know. No foreigner calling here is allowed to continue his journey without putting his fists to mine. So pick out your best man and match him against me on the spot. Otherwise you will find to your sorrow that if you defy my laws you will be brought by main force to obey them.'

His high-handed manner aroused them to fury, and Polydeuces, who took his threat as a personal affront, stepped forward at once to champion his friends.

'Enough!' he said. 'Whoever you may be, let us have no more of this parade of violence. You have stated your rules and we accept them. Here I am, ready to meet you of my own free will.'

Polydeuces, son of Zeus and Leda, was more than a match for Amycus, and after exchanging punches with the king he finally "landed him a lightning blow above the ear and smashed the bones inside." Amycus then collapsed on his knees in agony, and in a moment he was dead. The Bebryces were enraged by this and attacked Polydeuces, but his shipmates, including his brother Castor, stood by him with their swords drawn and fought off the barbarians until the enemy fled in disarray. The Argonauts then pillaged the cattle-yards and sheepfolds of the Bebryces, after which they slaughtered the animals for their victory feast, which Apollonius describes at the conclusion of his account of this adventure:

> They stayed there through the night, tended their wounded and with an offering to the immortal gods prepared a mighty feast. Nobody fell asleep by the wine-bowl and the blazing sacrifice. They crowned their golden heads with bay from the tree on the shore round which they had cast their hawsers, and in harmony with Orpheus' lyre they sang a song in praise of Poydeuces, Therapnean son of Zeus. Their music charmed the windless shore.
>
> When the sun came up from the world's end to light the dewy hills and wake the shepherds, they loosed their hawsers from the trunk of the bay-tree, and after stowing in the ship all of their booty that might be of use, they sailed up the swirling Bosphorus before the wind.

The supposed grave of King Amycus was pointed out along this coast in antiquity, and the French scholar Lechavalier, writing in the late eighteenth century, found it curious that Gyllius failed to identify it with the Giant's Grave on the hilltop to the north of Beykoz. On the spot where King Amycus was killed there grew up an *insana laurus*, an insane bay tree, which resembled Banquo's "insane root which takes the reason prisoner."

Beykoz is the only village on the Bosphorus that still has a dalyan in its harbor. Here, Dionysius Byzantius, Gyllius and Evliya Çelebi agree, is the one place on the Bosphorus where swordfish are caught. Evliya gives a lively account of the method, which is still used today by the fishermen who operate the *dalyan* in Beykoz:

There is in Beykoz a *dalyan*, or structure for hanging the swordfish; it is composed of five or six masts, on the highest of which sits a man who keeps a lookout for the fish that come in from the Black Sea. When he sees them drawing near, he throws a stone into the sea to frighten them, wherein he succeeds so well that they all take the direction of the harbor, where they think to find security, but fall into the nets laid for them in the water. The nets being closed, on warning from the man sitting in the lookout, the fishermen flock round to kill them without their being able to make any resistance with their swords. The fish if boiled with garlic and herbs is excellent.

After leaving the *iskele* at Beykoz the ferry crosses the huge bay formed by the Bosphorus as the stream changes direction from southeast to southwest. Near the southern end of the bay we pass İncirköy, Figtree Village, which is at the end of the charming valley of Sultaniye Deresi, where Beyazit II established extensive gardens. Evliya tells us that Murat III built an imperial kiosk here on the shore of the Bosphorus, installing in it a cupola, decorated with frescoes, that Osman Paşa had brought back from a victorious campaign in Persia. As Evliya describes the frescoes in the cupola, now vanished: "Painters are astonished that the pictures have suffered no injury from the air of the sea after so many years. All creatures between heaven and earth are here painted, for the most part in hunting parties."

Just beyond İncirköy the ferry stops at the *iskele* of Paşabahçe, the Pasha's Garden. This village takes its name from Hezar Para Ahmet Paşa, Grand Vezir of Sultan İbrahim, who planted extensive gardens here in preparation for erecting a palace. But when İbrahim was deposed by the Janissaries in 1648, the mob dragged Ahmet Paşa to the Hippodrome and literally tore him to pieces. Thenceforth he was known as Hezar Para, or Ahmet Paşa "of the Thousand Pieces." The village mosque is an undistinguished structure built in 1763 for Mustafa III. On the seashore is the Paşabahçe glass factory, world famous for its fine crystal and glassware; guided tours of the factory can be arranged, and there is an outlet shop in the lobby. At the southern end of the village there is a large distillery for making *rakı*, the anise-based national drink of Turkey.

From Paşabahçe a road leads inland from the Bosphorus. One branch of this road leads to Polonezköy, the Polish Village, a distance of about 25 kilometers. This pretty little village was founded in 1856 by the Polish Prince Adam Czartoryski, who received a grant of land from Sultan Abdülmecit for having commanded a detachment of emigre Polish soldiers in the Ottoman Army during the Crimean War. Their descendants continue to live in the village to the present day, still speaking Polish and retaining the cultural traditions of their ancestors, though many of them have intermarried with other Christian minorities in Istanbul. The village, with its Roman Catholic church and well constructed houses surrounded by carefully tended farms and orchards, appears to have been transplanted from Eastern Europe of an earlier era, a serene little oasis amidst the bleakness of the Bithynian hills. Rooms with full board can be rented in the village, which is renowned for its good Polish cooking, particularly pork and boar meat, and horses are available for riding.

Another branch of the road leads after a drive of some 80 kilometers to Şile on the Black Sea, a village that has now become a summer resort, with a magnificent beach of white sand that stretches westward for miles. The village is very picturesquely situated on a rocky promontory above the sea, with the ruins of a fourteenth-century Genoese fortress on an islet in the little harbor. On the beach a kilometer or so west of the village is the Kumbaba Motel, where excavations have unearthed ancient Greek columns, capitals and other architectural fragments, all of which are still lying around in the dunes. This has been identified as the site of ancient Calpe, a Greek colony on the Euxine that was probably founded around the same time as Byzantium, in the seventh century BC. Calpe is mentioned by Xenophon in his *Anabasis,* or The March Up-Country, an account of an epic journey made by an army of Greek mercenaries in western Asia during the years

401-399 BC. The Ten Thousand set out from Sardis in 401 BC in the service of Cyrus the Younger, who was attempting to usurp the throne of his brother, the Persian king, Artaxerxes II. Cyrus was killed at Cunaxa, north of Babylon, after which the Ten Thousand began their long march home under the command of Xenophon. The last stage of their journey brought them along the Black Sea coast of Asia Minor to Calpe, where they spent the winter of 400-399 BC. While in Calpe they defeated a Bithynian force that attempted to dislodge them, and then the following spring they crossed the Bosphorus to Byzantium, where they threatened to sack the city before they were given a subsidy to continue on their journey. Some distance westward along the beach from Kumbaba there is a great cavern known as Xenophon's Cave, where the Ten Thousand are supposed to have sheltered during their winter at Calpe. An exploration of the cave in the 1950s did in fact turn up a number of ancient Greek objects, including weapons dating from the time of the Ten Thousand.

The next village beyond Paşabahçe is Çubuklu, a pleasant hamlet in a verdant setting. In Byzantine times this was known as Eirenaion, or Peaceful, and it had a very famous monastery founded in 420 by St. Alexander for his order of Akoimetai, the Unsleeping, who prayed in relays throughout the day and night. Half a century later a branch of this order was installed in the newly founded monastery of St. John of Studius in Constantinople, where they won renown for their piety and scholarship. Evliya Çelebi tells an amusing story of how the village acquired its present Turkish name:

Beyazit II, having brought his son, the future Selim I, from Trebizond to Constantinople, gave him in this place in a fit of anger eight strokes with a cane (*çubuk*), which strokes were prophetic of the years of his reign. At the same time he said to him, 'Boy, don't be angry, these eight strokes shall fructify during the eight years of your reign,' Selim stuck the dry cane into the ground, praying to heaven that it might strike root and bear fruit. Şeyh Kara Şemseddin and Beyazit himself said, 'Amen'; the cane began to take root and even now bears cornels, five of which weigh a

114 *ANADOLUKAVAĞI TO ANADOLUHİSARI*

Hekimbaşı Salih Efendi Yalısı

Amcazade Hüseyin Paşa Yalısı

drachma, as large as the size of dates from Medina. Selim, having ascended the throne and conquered Egypt, beautified this place.

Beyond Çubuklu the shore curves sharply westward as we approach the upper end of the Narrows. On the hillside above are the beautiful woods known as Çubuklu Korusu, in the midst of which we see the cylindrical tower of the Hidiv Kasrı, one of the landmarks of this stretch of the Bosphorus. This is the palace of Abbas Hilmi Paşa, the last Ottoman Khedive of Egypt, erected around 1900; for an edifice of that late date in Ottoman architecture it has considerable charm. Its western facade overlooking the Bosphorus is semicircular, with a handsome marble columned porch and a semicircular hall within, surmounted by the cylindrical tower and a charming loggia on the roof. The Turkish Touring and Automobile Club has recently restored the palace and redecorated it superbly in its original Art Nouveau style, and it now serves as a luxury hotel and restaurant.

As we round the point at the entrance to the Narrows we pass the Rasim Paşa Yalısı, a nineteenth-century Ottoman mansion. The ferry then brings us to the *iskele* of Kanlıca, a pleasant village at the northern end of the Narrows opposite Emirgân. In Byzantine times the village was known as Glaros, or Seagull, and its small harbor was called Phrixos, in honor of the mythical hero who flew to Colchis on the golden fleeced ram. Kanlıca has, since the time of Evliya at least, been famous for its delicious yogurt, which is served in the little restaurants around the very attractive plane-tree shaded square by the *iskele*. At the far side of the square is the İskender Paşa Camii, a minor work of Sinan, built in 1559-60 for a vezir of Süleyman the Magnificent. The mosque is of the very simplest type, with a wooden porch and a flat roof, the latter replacing its original wooden dome. The founder's *türbe* is nearby. Evliya mentions İskender Paşa Camii in his description of Kanlıca:

It has nearly two thousand houses with gardens and fine *yalı*s. There are no Infidels, but altogether seven quarters of Muslims and a total of seven mosques and *mescit*s. The first is that of İskender Paşa at the head of the landing-place, built by one of the vezirs of Süleyman, a square building with a wooden roof covered with lead and a minaret, the work of Sinan. There are also two schools for boys, a school for reading the traditions, another for reading the Koran, a *han*, but no kitchen for the poor, and but one bath. In this bath is a lion carved in marble in so wonderful a manner that it appears to be alive. The milk and yogurt of this place are famous.

After leaving the *iskele* we pass the Ethem Pertev Yalısı, a very pretty seaside mansion that appears to date from the early nineteenth century. We then pass Kanlıca Bay, the ancient Phrixos, into which flows the Kavacık Deresi, a stream that has been identified as the Glarissa of antiquity. We then pass under the Fatih Sultan Mehmet Köprüsü once again, and then just beyond the bridge we see the rust-red Hekimbaşı Salih Efendi Yalısı, a very handsome mansion dating from the late eighteenth century or the early nineteenth. Only the central section of the *yalı* and its right wing remain, the left wing having been demolished.

A short distance beyond this we see the pathetic remains of the oldest and most historic *yalı* on the Bosphorus, a rose-red ruin tottering on rotting corbels at the lip of the sea. This is the Amcazade Hüseyin Paşa Köprülü Yalısı, built in 1698, although all that remains is just this central pavilion, the two wings having vanished. The *yalı* was built for Hüseyin Paşa, who served as Grand Vezir under Mustafa II (1695-1703). Hüseyin Paşa was the fourth of five members of the Köprülü family to serve as Grand Vezir, having succeeded his uncle and two of his cousins (*amcazade*). As Josef von Hammer writes of Hüseyin Paşa in his monumental *History of the Ottoman Empire*:

He was the fourth Köprülü endowed with the highest authority of the Empire, and like his relatives he showed himself capable of supporting its weight. After his uncle Mehmet Köprülü the Cruel and his cousins Ahmet the Statist and Mustafa the Virtuous, he well deserved the surname of the Wise. Unfortunately he remained all too short a time on the stage where his high qualities had placed him, fully capable as he was of retarding if not altogether forestalling the decadence of the Empire, from which he disappeared like a meteor after having given rise to the highest hopes.

The height of Hüseyin Paşa's career came in 1698-99, when he represented Mustafa II in the negotiations between the Ottoman Empire and the European powers that led to the Peace of Carlowitz. The final articles of this peace treaty were signed at the newly built Köprülü Yalısı on the Bosphorus on 26 January 1699, an agreement that historians consider to be the turning point in the Ottoman penetration of Europe, for thenceforth the Turkish wave receded.

This surviving central pavilion of the *yalı* has a central dome with spacious bays on three sides, with a continuous row of low windows on its seaward periphery letting in the cool breezes and providing views of the Bosphorus in all directions. This pavilion was renowned for its interior decoration, particularly the exquisite and elaborate molding and painting of ceilings and walls with arabesques, geometrical designs and floral garlands; equally lovely was a long series of panels above the windows, each with a vase of different flowers. During the early years of the twentieth century an attempt to rescue this unique room was made by the Society of the Friends of Istanbul, who published a sumptuous album of hand-gilded and colored plates with a preface by Pierre Loti and descriptive text by H. Saladin. Since then, however, the *yalı* has been totally neglected and is now in the last stages of decay, and if drastic measures are not taken in the near future it will very soon vanish, and with it will be gone a very precious heritage of Bosphorean architecture.

A little farther along we pass the Zaim Mustafa Paşa Yalısı, a handsome Ottoman mansion of the early nineteenth century, its central section on the upper floor projecting out over the sea on corbels. Farther along, as we pass the northern end of the village of Anadoluhisarı, we see a series of old *yalı*s, most of them apparently of the early nineteenth century, a number of them badly in need of repair.

The Asian shore of the middle Bosphorus was once particularly rich in *yalıs*, although some of the finest of these have been destroyed by fire in recent decades, such as the historic Cenani Yalısı in Kanlıca, which burned down in 1976. One of the first travellers to mention these *yalıs* seems to have been Byron, who in Canto V of *Don Juan* writes that "Each villa on the Bosphorus seems a scene/ New painted, or a pretty opera scene." This reminds one that these old *yalıs*, many of them half-ruined and some abandoned, their wooden walls faded into pale greys and browns, their grounds neglected and overgrown, were once brightly painted and embowered in lush and brilliant gardens, such as those that Julia Pardoe writes of in *The Beauties of the Bosphorus*, published in 1838, evoking a way of life that has now almost vanished in Istanbul.

The shores of the Bosphorus are a study - not only for their beauty, but because... of the dwellings that fringe them.... Thus, as the light caique of the observer skims over the ripple, the circumstances of almost every householder on the Bosphorus may be ascertained by the appearance of his dwelling. The residence of the favorite and the courtier is indeed a 'wide extensive building,' over whose front is 'bespent a deal of gilding and various hues'. The lattices of the harem are gaily painted, the terraces are bright with flowers, the marble steps against which the blue ripple chafes in the sunshine are thronged with attendants, and the caique that awaits its owner at the base is like a fairy bark, glittering with gold and crimson. Arabesques adorn the walls, and pretty kiosks peep from amid the leaves of the tall trees of the extensive gardens; the perfume of flowers and the sound of music come blended along the water.... When it is remembered that these houses are backed by a chain of fertile and well wooded hills, forming a succession of gardens and pleasure grounds, and are washed by the rapid current of the Bosphorus, it will be readily appreciated that they present a coup-d'oeil probably unique.... In many instances the buildings are raised along the extreme edge of the shore, and are unprotected even by a terrace; and the upper storeys generally projecting beyond the basement, they hang over the water in a singular manner.... Not the least beauty of these singular residences consists in their hanging terraces, frequently latticed in for the convenience of the harem, which makes the Bosphorus fragrant with the breath of flowers... The interior of these interesting dwellings is generally fitted up with much taste, and always with a careful regard to cheerfulness. The walls are painted in frescoes, with landscapes, fruits, or flowers; and the ceilings are always beautifully ornamented. In short, they are as fanciful, and almost as frail, as fairy palaces.

Here we have reached the narrowest point of the Bosphorus, some 750 meters wide between the opposing continental shores, with the great fortress of Rumelihisarı looming above the European side of the strait. Then on the Asian side of the strait we see the much smaller fortress of Anadoluhisarı, with the old houses and *yalı*s of the village clustering around it beside the Göksu, the northernmost of the two streams that make up the Sweet Waters of Asia. Then the ferry brings us to the *iskele* of Anadoluhisarı, directly under the walls of the old fortress.

CHAPTER EIGHT

ANADOLUHİSARI TO ÜSKÜDAR

The fortress of Anadoluhisarı is also known in Turkish as Güzelce, or the Charming One, a name that it well deserves, particularly on a late afternoon in summer when its crenellated walls and towers are mirrored in the deep blue waters of the Bosphorus.

The fortress was built c. 1394 by Beyazit I, at the beginning of his eight-year siege of Constantinople. Beyazit was known as Yıldırım, or Lightning, from the speed with which he marched his armies back and forth between victorious campaigns in Europe and Asia. In Marlowe's *Tamburlaine* he introduces himself thus:

> Dread Lord of Affricke, Europe and Asia,
> Great King and conqueror of Grecia,
> The Ocean, Terrene, and the cole-blacke sea.
> The high and highest Monarke of the world.

Beyazit met his match in Tamurlane, whose Mongol horde crushed Yıldırım's army at the battle of Ankara on 28 July 1402. Beyazit was taken alive by Tamurlane and died soon afterwards in ignominious captivity, apparently caged by his conqueror as if he were a wild beast that had been taken on the hunt. This is the scene we find later in Marlowe's play, when Tamurlane enters in triumph, along with "two Moores drawing Baiazeth in his cage, and his wife following him."

Beyazit's death abruptly ended the first Turkish siege of Constantinople, and the Byzantines gained a respite of half a century before Mehmet II renewed the assault against Byzantium. When he did so the young Sultan restored and possibly enlarged Anadoluhisarı while he was building the great fortress of Rumeli-

ANADOLUKAVAĞI TO ÜSKÜDAR 121

hisarı across the Bosphorus, so that the two forts between them would cut off Constantinople from the Black Sea.

The fortress is a small one, consisting of a keep and its surrounding wall together with an outer barbican, now partly demolished, guarded by three towers. It has been suggested that only the keep and its wall were built by Beyazit, with the barbican and its three towers added by Mehmet II in 1452. On the picturesque street that borders the fortress beside the Bosphorus we see one of the city's very few surviving *namazgâh*s, or open-air mosques; it consists simply of a *mihrap* and *mimber*, both made of stone, standing at one end of a grassy plot of ground surrounded by low walls. There is no inscription to date the *namazgâh*, but since it is not mentioned by Evliya Çelebi it can be no earlier than 1680; but it is listed in the *Hadikat* of Hafız Hüseyin Ayvansarayi, and so it was erected before c. 1780. According to Evliya, Mehmet II also built a mosque in Anadoluhisarı, but no trace of this remains. As Evliya writes in his description of Anadoluhisarı:

At the mouth of the small river Göksu on the sea-shore is a stronghold on the rocks built by Mehmet II; it is very small, and of but a thousand paces in circumference, with a gate opening to the west. Inside is a house for the commander, whose garrison numbers two hundred; the guns are pointed to the opposite shore of the Canal, where this castle is faced by Rumelihisarı. Before the castle is but one mosque, that of Mehmet II, and no other monument; the suburbs consist of a thousand and eighty houses, great palaces and *yalı*s, which however are much exposed to the sun in the afternoon. There are no Infidels or Jews, but all Muslims; besides the mosque just mentioned, there are some *mescit*s, and seven schools for boys, a small bath, and twenty shops, besides a great many gardens and vineyards.

Evliya then goes on to describe the river Göksu, the Heavenly Stream:

The Göksu is a river resembling the spring of life, which flows from

122 ANADOLUKAVAĞI TO ÜSKÜDAR

Anadoluhisarı

Fountain near the Asian Valley of Sweet Waters, on the Bosphorus

Mount Alemdağ, and is adorned on both banks with gardens and mills. It is crossed by a wooden bridge, under which pass the boats of lovers, who come here to enjoy the delicious meadows; it is a place very much worth seeing. Jars, cups and pots are made of a reddish clay found here.

The wooden bridge described by Evliya has been replaced by a concrete structure, by which the shore road crosses the Göksu. The clay beds that he writes of are still used to make crude pottery, which is sold at several potters upstream from the bridge. And the boats that he mentions still pass under the bridge, some of them it would seem carrying lovers, though not usually those of the type that Evliya had in mind.

After leaving Anadoluhisarı the ferry goes only about 400 meters down the Bosphorus before stopping at the Küçüksu İskelesi. The *iskele* takes its name from the Küçüksu, the Little Stream, which flows into the Bosphorus about 300 meters south of the Göksu. The area between these two streams, together known as the Sweet Waters of Asia, was up until the 1960s still covered with meadows, scarlet with poppies in the spring, one of the most beautiful spots along the Bosphorus, now utterly spoiled by modern structures and their pollution.

Küçüksu was much beloved by the Ottoman sultans, who would come here in their *pazar kayık*s for a day's outing. In later Ottoman times it became a favorite resort on holidays, particularly for women ordinarily sequestered in *harem*s, who could here enjoy an afternoon in the open air in this arcadian setting. Miss Pardoe describes the scene in *The Beauties of the Bosphorus:*

The Valley of Guik-Suy, charmingly situated about midway of the Bosphorus and called by Europeans the Asian Sweet Waters, owes its charm and popularity... to the circumstances of its being intersected by a pretty stream of fresh water, which, after flowing along under the shadows of tall and leafy trees, finally mingles its pygmy ripples with the swifter waves of the channel. The Anadoli Hissari, or Castle of Asia, stands upon its margin, and painfully recalls the mind to the darker and

Musicians at the Asian Valley of Sweet Waters

Küçüksu: Küçüksu Kasrı

sterner realities of life; or the visitor to Guiuk-Suy might fancy himself in Arcadia, so lovely is the locality.

On Fridays (the Mohammedan Sabbath), the valley is thronged with holiday-keeping idlers; and here the Frank traveller may see more of the habits and morale of the Turkish women than he can hope to do elsewhere; for here, being on Asiatic ground, they appear to feel more at home, and less trammelled by the restrictions of their creed than in any other environ of the capital; their yashmacs [head scarves] are less scrupulously arranged, they are more accessible to strangers, and they do the honors of their lovely valley with a gentle courtesy extremely pleasing.

All ranks alike frequent this sweet and balmy spot. The Sultanas move along in quiet stateliness over the greensward in their gilded arabas, drawn by oxen glittering with foil, and covered with awnings of velvet, heavy with gold embroidery and fringes; the light carriages of the Pashas' harems roll rapidly past, decorated with flashing draperies, the horses gaily caparisoned, and the young beauties within pillowed on satins and velvets, and frequently screened by shawls of immense value; while the wives of many of the Beys, the Effendis, and the Emirs, leave their *araba*s, and seated on Persian carpets under the leafy canopy of the superb maple-trees which abound in the valley, amuse themselves for hours, the elder ladies with their pipes, and the younger ones with their hand-mirrors; greetings innumerable take place on all sides; and the itinerant confectioners and water-vendors reap a rich harvest....

Wallachian and Jewish musicians are common; and the extraordinary length of time during which they will dwell upon a single note, with their heads thrown back, their mouths open, and their eyes fixed, and then follow it up with a whole sentence, rapidly and energetically uttered, is most singular. But these oriental troubadours are not without their rivals in their admiration of the veiled beauties who surround them; conjurors, improvvisatori, story-tellers, and Bulgarian dancers are there also, to seduce away a portion of their audience; while the interruptions caused by fruit, sherbet and water-vendors, are incessant. They are however, the most popular of all; and a musician, whose talent is known and acknowledged, seldom fails to spend a very profitable day at the Asian Sweet Waters on every occasion of festival.

ANADOLUKAVAĞI TO ÜSKÜDAR

Of the structures built there by the sultans only a small palace and a fountain remain to evoke something of the atmosphere of pleasure parties on the Sweet Waters of Asia in Ottoman times.

Küçüksu Kasrı, which is on the edge of the Bosphorus just downstream from the *iskele*, is a pretty little palace in the Turkish rococo style. It was erected for Sultan Abdülmecit in 1856-57 by Nikogos Balyan, replacing the last of a series of imperial kiosks on the same site, the earliest dating back to 1752. Abdülmecit at first used Küçüksu Kasrı only as a *pied-a-terre* on day-trips from Dolmabahçe Palace, and so the palace here did not include bedrooms in its original design. But several chambers were converted into bedrooms in the late nineteenth century, when Küçüksu was used to house visiting dignitaries, a function it continued to serve in the first half-century of the Republic. The palace was restored in the 1970s and is now open as a museum.

Just beside the palace to its left on the shore is the Küçüksu Çeşmesi, one of the most beautiful baroque fountains in Istanbul. The fountain was built in 1796 for Selim III, who dedicated it to his beloved mother, the Valide Sultan Mihrişah. The fountain is square with upturned eaves and colonettes set in its corners, with the spigots and their basins framed in round arches. The Sultan's name and the date of foundation of the fountain are given in a long calligraphic chronogram of thirty-two lines by the poet Hatif inscribed across all four faces of the *çeşme*, ending with these lines:

> And our course wishes to be of this water now,
> And to be as tall as a cypress tree, a fragile beauty in the
> meadow;
> Hatif, tell us a date worthy of this soul-caressing fountain:
> Küçüksu gave to this continent brilliance and light.

Miss Pardoe also writes of this fountain in *The Beauties of the Bosphorus*, once again describing the Sweet Waters of Asia in a holiday mood:

Valide Sultan Mihrişah Çeşmesi

128 *ANADOLUKAVAĞI TO ÜSKÜDAR*

The Fountain of Guiuk-Suy stands in the midst of a double avenue of trees, which fringe the border of the Bosphorus. It is built of delicate white marble, is extremely elegant in design and elaborately ornamented with arabesques. The spot which it adorns is a point of reunion for the fair idlers of the valley, when the evening breeze upon the channel renders this portion of the glen more cool and delicious than that in which they pass the earlier hours of the day; and is only separated from it by the stream already named, which is traversed by a heavy wooden bridge.

The whole *coup-d'oeil* is charming; slaves hurry hither and thither, carrying water from the fountain to their respective mistresses, in covered crystal goblets, or vases of wrought silver. Fruit-merchants pass and repass with amber-colored grapes and golden melons; Sclavonian musicians collect a crowd about them, which disperses the next moment to throng round a gang of Bedouin tumblers; serudjhes gallop over the soft grass in pursuit of their employers; carriages come and go noiselessly along the turf at the beck of their fair occupants; a fleet of caiques dance upon the ripple, ready to convey a portion of the revellers to their homes on the European shore; and the beams of the bright sun fall full on the turreted towers of the Castle of Europe, on the opposite side of the channel, touching them with gold, and contrasting yet more powerfully their long and graceful shadows upon the water.

Beyond Küçüksu the shore curves southwest and then west as the Bosphorus bends sharply below the Narrows, then bending sharply in the opposite direction around Kandilli Burnu. Here the ferry passes close along the Asian shore on its way from Küçüksu to its next stop at the Kandilli İskelesi, which is about 150 meters eastward of the promontory. En route from Küçüksu to Kandilli we pass two of the oldest and finest *yalıs* on the Bosphorus, which we can look at closely as the ferry passes close under their seaside facades.

The first of these, just beyond the beach at Küçüksu, is the Kıbrıslı Mustafa Emin Paşa Yalısı. Built originally about 1760 but added to and redecorated later, its facade on the Bosphorus is over sixty meters long, mostly of one story but with a central part of

ANADOLUKAVAĞI TO ÜSKÜDAR 129

Kıbrıslı Yalısı

Ostrorog Yalısı

two. The rooms are arranged with great symmetry around three great halls, rather than the usual two; of these the eastern one is perhaps the most beautiful, paved in marble with a marble fountain in the center under a vaulted ceiling decorated with exquisite moldings and painted panels of bowls of flowers; to north and south slender wooden columns with Corinthian capitals divide the central space from two bays, one giving directly onto the sea, the other providing the entrance from the garden. Four superbly proportioned rooms open from the hall, two overlooking the Bosphorus, two the garden. Still farther to the east is an enormous ballroom and a charming greenhouse with a pebble mosaic and a great marble pool with a curious fountain. The *harem* occupied the western wing of the house and was the oldest part of it; unfortunately it was demolished in 1970. Descendants of the Grand Vezir Mustafa Emin Paşa continue to live in the *yalı*.

A short distance beyond the Kıbrıslı Yalısı we see the beautiful red Ostrorog Yalısı, also known as the Kırmızı (Red) Yalı. The *yalı* was built around 1790 by the Ostrorogs, a noble French-Polish family that had connections with the Ottoman Empire going back to the sixteenth century. The last of the line, Count Jean Ostrorog, died in the *yalı* in 1975. The lower room at the left corner of the *yalı* was used by the French writer Pierre Loti during his residence in Istanbul in the 1890s; his two most famous novels, *Aziyade* and *Desenchantees*, are set in *yalı*s along the Anatolian shore of the Bosphorus, with scenes along the Sweet Waters of Asia.

The Kıbrıslı and Ostrorog *yalı*s still retain their beautiful gardens on the Bosphorus. The present writer has been privileged to attend garden parties at both of these *yalı*s, and in both cases the festivities were lighted by a full moon, when the Bosphorus is its most beautiful, particularly in early June, the traditional time for these fetes. Miss Pardoe describes the scene in *The Beauties of the Bosphorus:*

The Bosphorus wears the most animated expression early in June, when

ANADOLUKAVAĞI TO ÜSKÜDAR 131

the trees are in full foliage, and every leaf is redolent of life, ere the heats have weathered the herbiage, and when a light southerly wind is wafting hundreds of vessels up the strait toward the Black Sea, the inner tiers almost touching the houses with their spars; while all the caiques are plying busily between the city and the villages on the channel, laughter is ringing out on the clear air, roses blooming along the banks, and the waters are buoyant with life and motion, and adding to the magic of the landscape.

But to be seen in all its beauty, it should be looked upon by moonlight. Then it is that the occupants of the spacious mansions which overhang its waters enjoy to the fullest perfection the scene around them. The glare of noonday reveals too fully the colors of the picture, and the garish sun withers as it shines; while the deep, purple, star-encrusted sky, the pure moonlight, and the holy quiet of evening, lend to it, on the contrary, a mysterious indistinctness which doubles its attraction.

The inhabitants of the capital are conscious of this fact; and during the summer months, when they occupy their marine villas, one of their favorite recreations is to seat themselves upon their seaward terraces to enjoy the passing music of the caiques which skim over the ripple, freighted with amateur minstrels gliding from house to house, and warbling their good-night to each, to the accompaniment of a guitar; or in listening to the evening hymns of the seamen on board the Italian and Greek vessels anchored in the strait; amused at intervals by the rolling of a huge shoal of porpoises on their way to the harbor (where they frequently abound), gamboling in the moonlight, and plunging in the waves with a sound like thunder; while in the distance, loom out the dark mountains of the Asian coast, casting their dusky shadows far across the water; and close beside them are the quivering summits of the tall trees on the edge of the channel, sparkling like silver, and lending the last touch of loveliness to a landscape, perhaps unparalleled in the world.

After leaving the *iskele* at Kandilli the ferry rounds Kandilli Burnu, where the Bosphorus changes course from southwest to south-southeast. The velocity of the water streaming around the point is the highest on the Asian shore of the Bosphorus, usually four to five knots, even higher when the north wind is blowing strongly, known to Bosphorus mariners as the Devil's Current. The deepest point in the Bosphorus is in the center of the channel off Kandilli Burnu, where there is a trough 110 meters in depth.

Some 900 meters beyond Kandilli Burnu the ferry stops at the *iskele* of Vaniköy, a little village opposite Arnavutköy on the European shore. On the hilltop above Vaniköy we see the tower and telescope dome of Kandilli Rasathanesi, an astronomical observatory and meteorological station. The Rasathane has an interesting collection of the instruments used by Takiuddin, the great sixteenth-century Turkish astronomer, whose work was on a par with the famous astronomers of his time in western Europe. He was also a renowned astrologer, too good, in fact, for his observation of the supernova, or new star, of 1576 led him to predict a great disaster for the Ottoman Empire, which came true when the Grand Vezir Sokollu Mehmet Paşa was assassinated three years later, a baleful forecast that led the Ulema, or religious hierarchy, to destroy Takiuddin's observatory.

No trace remains of the imperial kiosks and gardens that once adorned Kandilli and Vaniköy. Evliya describes these in his section on the pleasant walks south of the Sweet Waters of Asia, and he also tells an interesting tale about Sultan Selim I, the Grim, and his son and successor, Süleyman the Magnificent.

South of this place [the Sweet Waters of Asia] is Kandilli, the kiosk of which was built by Murat III; Murat IV, much delighted by the air and the view, spent here a great deal of his time. It is a delicious garden, adorned with many pleasure-houses. The mountains behind are laid out in vineyards. The garden is ruled by an Usta [Foreman] and one hundred Bostancıs [Gardeners]. South of it Mehmet IV made a present to Vani Efendi [head of the Ulema] of a place called Papazkarası (the Priest's Lands) as an imperial gift. The walk near this place is called Kule Bahçesi (Tower Garden). Selim I, having in a fit of anger ordered his son Süleyman to be put to death, the Bostancıbaşı [Head Gardener] feigned to obey the Sultan's command, but killed another boy instead of the Prince, whom he shut up during three years in this tower. Selim on his return from Egypt, feeling his end to be drawing near, reproached the Bostancıbaşı as the cause of his being about to die without heirs. The Bostancıbaşı kissed the ground, and brought Süleyman from his tower to Sultan Selim's presence, who caught him eagerly in his arms. The Bostancıbaşı was rewarded with the governorship of Egypt, and Süleyman built on the site of the tower, where he had been shut up for three years, a magnificent building nine stories high, everywhere finished with waterpipes and fountains. There exists here a wonderfully tall cypress tree, which Sultan Süleyman planted with his own hand. Of the different delicious fruits of this garden, the figs are the best.

The huge building with twin conical-capped towers on the shore south of Vaniköy is the Kuleli Naval Officers' Training College. The original military training school and barracks here were built c. 1800 by Selim III, part of his program to reform and modernize the Ottoman armed forces. The original building served as a military hospital in 1855-56, at the end of the Crimean War, when it was one of the two medical institutions in Istanbul under the supervision of Florence Nightingale, the other and larger one being the Selimiye barracks in Üsküdar.

Kuleli is believed to stand on the site of a famous convent founded by the Empress Theodora, wife of the Emperor Justinian. This institution was called Metanoia, or Repentance, and was used to house reformed prostitutes, a project in which Theodora was deeply interested, since she herself had been a harlot in her youth. Justinian's court chronicler Procopius writes ironically of Metanoia in his *Secret History,* a scathing and sometimes bizarre account of life behind the scenes in the Great Palace of Byzantium.

Theodora also devoted considerable attention to the punishment of women caught in carnal sin. She picked up more than five hundred harlots in the Forum, who earned a miserable existence by selling themselves for three obols, and sent them to the opposite mainland, where they were locked up in the convent called Repentance. Some of them, however, threw them-

134 ANADOLUKAVAĞI TO ÜSKÜDAR

Kandilli: *Yalı*s

Kuleli Naval Officer's Training College

ANADOLUKAVAĞI TO ÜSKÜDAR 135

selves from the parapets at night and thus freed themselves from an undesired salvation.

The ferry stops next at the *iskele* of Çengelköy, the Village of the Hooks, or Anchors. The origin of Çengelköy's curious name is explained by Evliya: "This is called the Village of Hooks, because at the time of the conquest of Constantinople by Mehmet II, certain old anchor-hooks of the time of the Byzantine Emperors were found here." The seaside village square of Çengelköy is very pleasant, surrounded by a number of restaurants with views down the lower Bosphorus to its confluence with the Golden Horn, with the domes and spires of the monuments on the First Hill silhouetted on the skyline of Stamboul. On the south side of the village we see the rust-red Sadullah Paşa Yalısı, a very handsome seaside mansion dating from the late eighteenth century or the early nineteenth.

The ferry stops next at the *iskele* of Beylerbeyi, which has the same name as the splendid seaside palace just down the strait, almost directly under the first Bosphorus Bridge. The village was known in the medieval Byzantine period as Chrysokeramos, or the Golden Tiles, apparently because it had a remarkable church with gilded roof tiles. Later it was known to the Greeks as Stavros, a name that continued in use well into Ottoman times. The present name of the village stems from the fact that it was near the site of a palace built by Mehmet Paşa, who was Beylerbeyi, or Governor, of the Province of Rumeli during the reign of Murat III. Mehmet Paşa's residence was the first of a succession of kiosks, pavilions and palaces built in the vicinity of the village before the present Beylerbeyi Sarayı. Evliya mentions a number of these palaces in his description of the village:

A great number of the inhabitants are Greek; the palaces, many of which belong to the Sultan and vezirs, are very fine; the finest are those of Moanoğlu, of Beylerbeyi, and near it the imperial garden of Stavros; the kiosks and handsome buildings seen here are to be found in no other royal palace. But God knows, the foundation of this palace must have been laid under the constellation of Mars, because Sultan Murat IV, having fixed his abode here, issued many orders for the shedding of blood. Elias Paşa, who had raised a rebellion in Anatolia, and shut up in the passage of Pergamus, was brought into the Emperor's presence at this place, and executed with many others. The inhabitants are a noisy and quarrelsome people, but the place is well-built and cultivated. There are some three thousand and sixty houses of stone, some with upper stories, and some of one floor only. The mosque is in the middle of the marketplace.

The mosque mentioned by Evliya has been replaced by the present Beylerbeyi Camii, which is at the back of the village square by the *iskele*. This was built in 1778 for Sultan Abdülhamit I by Mehmet Tahir Ağa, by far the best of the Turkish baroque architects. The mosque is an attractive example of the Turkish baroque style, its dome arches arranged in an octagon, vigorously emphasized within and without, its *mihrap* in a projecting apse, richly decorated with an assortment of tiles of various periods ranging from the sixteenth century to the eighteenth. The *mihrap* and *Kuran kürsüsü* are unusually elegant and beautiful works, both of them in wood inlaid with ivory. The mosque has two minarets, the second one added later by Mahmut II. The lower part of each minaret consists of a base of square cross-section above which there is a bulbous foot, rather like a flattened bell jar; from this rises the fluted shaft, which has a single *şerefe*, or balcony, and an onion-like stone crown with a tall horned *alem*, or crescent-like symbol. This is the earliest appearance of this type of minaret, which, particularly the bulbous foot, became a characteristic feature in mosques of the late eighteenth century and on through the nineteenth century.

The shore road leads from the *iskele* to Beylerbeyi Sarayı, the largest and grandest Ottoman palace on the Asian shore of the Bosphorus.

The first sultan to reside on this site was Mahmut II, who

ANADOLUKAVAĞI TO ÜSKÜDAR 137

Beylerbeyi: Beylerbeyi Camii

Beylerbeyi: Beylerbeyi Sarayı

built a summer palace here that was destroyed by fire in the mid-nineteenth century. Miss Pardoe describes this earlier Palace of Beylerbeyi as it appeared during the last years of Mahmut's reign, some two decades before the present Dolmabahçe Sarayı became the principal residence of the imperial family and its entourage on the Bosphorus:

> The Sultan's summer-palace of Beglier Bey, on the Asiatic shore, is the most elegant object on the Bosphorus. It is an elegantly fronted and extensive edifice, stretching along the lip of the channel, whose waves wash its long and stately terraces of glittering marble, and sometimes penetrate into their latticed and mysterious recesses. The building is of wood; and the *harem* presents a line of gables perforated with long ranges of windows secured by most minute screens of gilded wood: the Salemliek, containing the State apartments, the private saloons of the Sultan, and the rooms occupied by the Imperial household, is an octagonal pile, of which the painted roof is surmounted by a crescent supporting a star, whose richly gilded points flash in the sunshine like lambent fire. The entire building is painted in white and pale gold; and it has rather the appearance of a fairy-palace, called into existence by enchantment, than the every-day work of human hands.

The present palace was built for Sultan Abdülaziz in 1861-65 by Sarkis Balyan, brother of Nikogos Balyan, architect of Dolmabahçe Sarayı. Beylerbeyi Sarayı was used mainly as a summer lodge and a residence for foreign dignitaries, the first being the Empress Eugenie of France at the time of her visit to Istanbul in 1869. Abdülhamit II spent the last years of his life here after his return from Thessalonika, where he had lived for four years after being deposed in 1908, and he died peacefully in Beylerbeyi Sarayı in 1918.

The palace is divided into the usual *harem* and *selamlık*. The building is in three stories, although only the upper two floors are visible along the Bosphorus facade. The ground floor houses the kitchens and other service departments; the state rooms and the imperial apartments are on the two upper floors, a total of twenty-six elegantly appointed chambers, including six grand salons, with a magnificent spiral staircase leading upwards from the reception hall that divides the *harem* from the *selamlık*. Beylerbeyi is as sumptuously furnished and decorated as Dolmabahçe; its adornments include Hereke carpets, chandeliers of Bohemian crystal, French clocks, vases from China, Japan, France and the imperial workshops at Yıldız Sarayı, which also manufactured all of the furniture, and it is adorned with frescoes and framed paintings by European artists, most notably Ayvasovski. The structures in the gardens behind the palace include the Mermer (Marble) Köşk, Sarı (Yellow) Köşk and Ahır (Stable) Köşkü. Two smaller kiosks flank the main facade of the palace along the sea, the southernmost one now standing almost directly under the Boğaziçi Köprüsü (Bosphorus Bridge).

After leaving the *iskele* at Beylerbeyi the ferry passes under the Bosphorus Bridge. Then some 750 meters beyond the bridge the ferry stops at the *iskele* in Kuzguncuk, the last station before Üsküdar on the Asian shore of the Bosphorus.

According to Evliya, the village "takes its name from a pious man Kuzgun Baba, who resided here in the time of Sultan Mehmet II." But it is more likely that the name of the village comes from the Turkish *kuzgun*, or "raven." Despite its close proximity to Üsküdar, Kuzguncuk still retains its village character, and it remains one of the most attractive and interesting communities on the Bosphorus. Like most of the villages on the Bosphorus, Kuzguncuk had a very diversified population. As Cengiz Bektaş notes in his sensitive and beautifully written article in Istanbul Magazine, recording the change in the ethnic composition of Kuzguncuk between 1914 and 1992:

The population of the village [in 1914] consisted of 70 Muslims, 250 Greeks, 1600 Armenians (including those in İcadiye), 400 Jews and four foreign households. There were three churches, two synagogues, one mosque and three fountains.... Now in June 1992, Kuzguncuk has a total population of fifteen thousand, including twenty-five Greeks, seventeen Jews and six Armenians.

There are now two mosques, Uryanizade Camii and Kuzguncuk Camii. The first of these is on the seashore upstream from the *iskele*, distinguished by its quaint wooden minaret; this was erected in the 1880s by Uryanizade Ahmet Esat Efendi, and rebuilt after a fire in the 1980s. The other mosque, Kuzguncuk Camii, was built in 1952; it stands on the main street of the village side-by-side with the Armenian church of Surp Kirkor Lusavoriç, which was erected in 1831 and rebuilt in 1861. The Greek Orthodox church of Ayios Panteleon was erected in 1831 and rebuilt in 1896; beside it there is an *ayazma* which has recently been rededicated. The other Greek church, dedicated to Ayios Yiorgios, is dated by an inscription to 1821. Another inscription records that Ayios Yiorgios was built on the site of an earlier church of Ayios Panteleon dating back to 550. Next to the church of Ayios Yiorgios is the larger of the two synagogues, erected in 1818; the other synagogue dates to 1886. The inner streets of the village, some of which still end in stepped streets, are lined with graceful old houses, many of them with delicately carved wooden balconies looking out through arcades. One particularly handsome stone house forming a corner has in its ground floor the very elegant shop of the village barber, Muzaffer Bey. Another old wooden house has had its main room converted into a little theater, where in the spring of 1991 the renowned Turkish playwright Güngör Dilmen, a resident of Kuzguncuk, put on a new version of his much acclaimed play, *I Anatolia*.

Cengiz Bektaş has recorded the reminiscences of a number of old residents of Kuzguncuk, some of whom have now passed away, their collective memories evoking a picture of what life was like in this Bosphorus village in times not long past. As he writes:

Today is Sunday 31 May... A short time ago I came back from a picnic at which the residents of Kuzguncuk were singing and dancing to the accompaniment of an accordion and guitar, and eating and drinking together. I sat down and began to write these lines, setting down these stories exactly as the natives of Kuzguncuk related them. And that's how I shall relate them to you.

Until 6/7 September [1955], İcadiye Caddesi, Kuzguncuk's main street, was closed to traffic at Easter (*panayır*). Carpets were laid out on the ground, flowers were scattered everywhere, *laterna*s (barrel organs) brought out, and dancing went on for three days and nights.

The festivities were described by Nazım's aunt, Sare Teyze, Kuzguncuk's oldest inhabitant.

'We grew up together. We were like brothers and sisters. We played together. We went in and out of each others houses. We would visit each other. Tables would be set for meals in the garden under the Judas trees.'

Glazier Koço, may his soul rest in peace, would put his hand on her shoulder and go on with the story:

'Weren't we like brothers, Barba? Our joys and sorrows all together... What times we had! Who can forget the *panayır* days! *Laterna*s were set up all over İcadiye. Everyone danced. Three days and three nights.'

Mrs. N. (Turkish): 'Our neigbors were a Madame Donna and a Madame Ester... We got on very well. They would allow us to attend their circumcision feasts. They would also invite us to their Feast of the Passover. They would come to celebrate the Sacrificial and Ramazan feasts with us... We got on very well with our Jewish and Greek neighbors. The women would make lace, sew and do embroidery. Sometimes they would sell their work. In the evenings we could hear music from their houses. They would play the violin or the piano. We would also hear the sound of an accordion. At sunset our neighbor Kenan Bey would play an improvisation on the *kanun*. Sometimes the fiddler would come and there would be great fun....'

In short people may have been poor, but Kuzguncuk was a place of neighborliness, companionship, love and affection.

CHAPTER NINE
ÜSKÜDAR

The ferry now brings us to the *iskele* at Üsküdar, the last stop on the Asian side of the Bosphorus.

Üsküdar was originally known as Chrysopolis, the City of Gold, a name that survived up until the twelfth century. Chrysopolis in antiquity was a suburb of Chalcedon, the modern Kadıköy, which is situated on the Asian shore of the Sea of Marmara just outside the mouth of the Bosphorus. According to tradition, both cities were founded c. 670 BC, a decade before the establishment of Byzantium. Chrysopolis, because of its fine natural harbor and its strategic position at the head of the strait, developed rapidly and soon surpassed Chalcedon in size and importance; it became the starting place for the great Roman roads that led from Byzantium into Asia, a convenient mustering place for military and commercial expeditions into Anatolia. Throughout the Byzantine period both Chrysopolis and Chalcedon were suburbs of Constantinople. But their sites were not well suited for defence, and on several occasions they were occupied and destroyed by invading armies while Constantinople remained safe behind its great walls. Thus there are no monuments of the Byzantine period in the Asian suburbs of the city. Chrysopolis and Chalcedon were taken by the Turks in the mid-fourteenth century, a hundred years or so before the fall of Constantinople. Chalcedon came to be called Kadıköy, the Town of the Judge (*kadı*), because it was the headquarters for the Chief Justice of the Ottoman Empire's Anatolian provinces. Chrysopolis became Üsküdar, a corruption of Scutari, the name by which the town was known from the late Byzantine period up until fairly recent times. This name dates from the twelfth century and derives from the imperial Byzantine palace of Scutarion, which stood on a promontory of the Asian shore directly across the strait from Sarayburnu.

During the Ottoman period Üsküdar was adorned with splen-

ÜSKÜDAR 143

did mosque complexes and other pious foundations. Almost all of these monuments are still standing, along many wooden houses of the late Ottoman period, although these have been disappearing rapidly in recent years. Nevertheless, Üsküdar still retains vestiges of its Ottoman past, and it has a much more Anatolian atmosphere than the imperial city across the strait, which has always been more cosmopolitan. Here again we can evoke a picture of Üsküdar in Ottoman times by reading Evliya Çelebi, who describes its inhabitants in Section 74 of his *Seyahatname:*

Scutari is a great place of passage, because all foreigners from Anatolia, Arabia, Persia and India, coming to Constantinople, pass through it.... This town consists of seventy quarters of Moslems, eleven of Greeks, and one of Jews, but no Franks [western Europeans]; it is not fortified.... A regiment of Janissaries mount guard. There are also veterans of the gunners, armorers and *sipahis*; a great number of noble and learned men have taken up their residence here.... The soldiers are of the first class, they dress in rich brocades. The other classes are of the rich divines, the fakirs, the boatmen, and the merchants, who dress according to their means in dolimans and ferajahs of cloth; as the greater part of them are Anatolians they speak the dialect of this province, but the gentlemen of the town speak in the purest way, and are poets and learned divines. The principal order of dervishes at Scutari being the Helveti, you find here a great number of musical people, who sing different songs of divine love (*ilahi*) in the established rhythm. The number of the fair sex of this town is very great, and poets have made of them the subject of a Şehrengiz, or town-revolt.... There are white cracknels, good roast meat, fresh *kaymak*, and sherbet with musk-raisins.

İskele Meydanı, the great square around the ferry station, has been the focal point of Üsküdar since the beginning of its history, a hive of activity, with hordes of people arriving and leaving at all hours of the day aboard the ferries and water taxis that cross the Bosphorus here. In Ottoman times this was the mustering place for the Sürre-i-Hümayun, the Sacred Caravan that each year departed for Mecca and Medina with its long train of pilgrims and its white camel bearing gifts from the Sultan to the Şerif of Mecca. Evliya was the Chief Imam of the Sürre-i-Hümayun that left for the holy cities in 1680, but he never returned, and is believed to have died and been buried in Cairo.

Looking to the left we see İskele Camii, the handsome mosque that dominates the scene from its terrace above the eastern end of the seaside square.

The mosque was built in 1547-48 by Sinan for the Princess Mihrimah Sultan, only daughter of Süleyman the Magnificent and wife of the Grand Vezir Rüstem Paşa. The exterior is very imposing because of its position high above the square and its great double porch, a curious projection of which covers a charming fountain. Professor Aptullah Kuran, in his book on the works of Sinan, points out that this is one of the first examples of the use of a double portico in Ottoman architecture. The outer porch has a penthouse roof and the inner one has five domed bays. Projecting from the center of the outer porch there is an extension covering a charming baroque fountain, erected in 1726 by Ahmet III, the Tulip King. The interior of the mosque is covered by a central dome supported by semidomes on the sides and in the direction of the *kıble*, with the absence of a fourth semidome at the rear leaving the prayer-room with a curiously truncated appearance.

The *külliye* of Mihrimah Sultan also includes a *medrese* and a primary school. The *medrese* is to the north of the mosque, a pretty building of the rectangular type, now used as a clinic. The primary school is behind the mosque, built on sharply rising ground so that it has picturesque supporting arches; it has been restored and is now a children's library.

We now walk around the landward side of İskele Meydanı and enter the main avenue of Üsküdar. Here we see on the left a supermarket housed in the remains of an ancient *hamam*. The owner calls it Sinan Hamam Çarşısı, thus ascribing it to Sinan; this is probably not so, though it certainly dates from his time. It was a double *hamam*, with one bath for men and the other for women,

Üsküdar: İskele Camii

Üsküdar: Şemsi Paşa Camii

but the main entrance chambers in both sections were demolished when the street was widened.

A little further on there is a curious mosque built by Nişancı Kara Davut Paşa toward the end of the fifteenth century. The interior is a broad and shallow room, with two sections side-by-side each covered by a dome, an arrangement unique in Istanbul.

Across the street and opening into the square is the large mosque complex called Yeni Valide Camii, built in 1708-10 for Ahmet III, who dedicated it to the memory of his mother, the Valide Sultan Rabia Gülnus Emetullah. The Valide Sultan was born Evmania Voria, daughter of a Greek priest in a village near Rethymnon on Crete. She was captured by the Turks when they took Rethymnon in 1645, when she was just three years old, after which she was taken to Istanbul and placed in the Harem of Topkapı Sarayı, given the name of Rabia Gülnus, the Rose of Spring. She eventually became one of the concubines of Mehmet IV, bearing him a son in 1664 and another the following year. Her first son succeeded to the throne in 1695 as Mustafa II, whereupon she became Valide Sultan. When Mustafa died in 1703 he was succeeded by his brother Ahmet III, her second son, and so she continued to rule the Harem in Topkapı Sarayı as Valide Sultan. When Rabia Gülnus died in 1708 Sultan Ahmet commissioned this mosque complex in her memory, burying her there in an ornate *türbe*. Her *türbe* is at the corner of the complex, a charming structure covered by a decorative metal grill instead of a roof, looking rather like an aviary. The mosque itself was built at the end of the classical period in Ottoman architecture, just before the baroque influence had come to enliven it. In plan it is a variant of the octagon-in-a-square theme, decorated with inferior tiles of late date. The *külliye* also includes a primary school, which is over the main gate, and an *imaret*, or free kitchen. The *imaret* is outside the gate, with a fountain at the corner; the *çeşme* is of later date than the rest of the *külliye* and is fully in the baroque style.

We now continue around the landward side of İskele Meydanı and make our way to its westward end, where we walk along the

ÜSKÜDAR

edge of the Bosphorus toward the broad cape at the lower end of the strait.

This brings us to Şemsi Paşa Camii, which Evliya calls "a pretty little mosque on the lip of the sea," one of the landmarks on the Asian shore of the Bosphorus at its lower end. This is one of the most delightful of the smaller mosque complexes of the city, built of glittering white stone and standing in a very picturesque location right at the water's edge. The complex was built by Sinan in 1580 for Şemsi Paşa, a vezir of the Isfendiyar family who traced his descent to the Selçuk sultans who ruled Anatolia before the rise of the Ottomans.

The *külliye* consists of the mosque, a *medrese*, and the *türbe* of the founder. The precinct wall of the *külliye* is almost rectangular in form, except for an L-shaped section at its northeast corner, where the *türbe* adjoins the quay, attached to the side of the mosque. The northern precinct wall along the quay has grilled windows opening into the courtyard, whose west side has at its center the *dershane*, or lecture-hall of the *medrese*, flanked on either side by two cells for students, with another cell adjacent to the northwest corner and five on the south side, all of them domed, followed by the cross-vaulted bay of the entrance portal. In front of the cells along the interior periphery of the courtyard is a portico covered by a penthouse roof carried on eighteen marble columns..

The mosque makes an angle of thirty-seven degrees with the east and west sides of the precinct, its entryway facing the northwest corner of the courtyard. An L-shaped penthouse porch extends around the front and right side of the mosque, with the minaret rising from a concealed base in the front right-hand corner of the building. The interior of the mosque is square in plan, with the room covered by a dome 8.2 meters in diameter with conces as squinches. Şemsi Paşa's cross-vaulted *türbe* opens off from the left side of the prayer room, from which it is separated only by a green grill, a most unusual and pretty feature.

We now continue along the Bosphorus on the esplanade of

the new Sahil Yolu. This takes us around the huge promontory where the Bosphorus turns south around the Asian shore opposite its confluence with the Golden Horn, after which it flows on into the Sea of Marmara. This last stretch of the Bosphorus, which is about two kilometers long and ranging in width from 1,800 to 2,000 meters, was known in Byzantine times as the Arm of St. George. This name came from the church of St. George of the Mangana, which stood on the shore of the First Hill just south of Saray- burnu. The great chain that the Byzantines stretched across the Bosphorus in times of siege extended from the base of this church to Kız Kulesi, or the Maiden's Tower, the islet we see some 200 meters off the coast at Salacak, the promontory of Üsküdar.

Kız Kulesi is also known in English as Leander's Tower. This comes from a mistaken notion that it is associated with the myth of Hero and Leander, which actually took place on the Hellespont. The Turkish name of the islet is derived from a legend concerning a princess who was confined there by her father, who had been warned by a seer that she was doomed to die from the bite of a serpent. But in spite of this a snake was smuggled out to the islet hidden in a basket of fruit, and when it bit the princess she died instantly. (The Turks are very taken by this legend, and have associated it with several towers and castles along their coasts.). According to the Byzantine chronicler Nicetas Choniates, the Emperor Manuel I Comnenus fortified the islet in the mid-twelfth century, using it to anchor the eastern end of the chain across the Bosphorus. Since then the islet has served in turn as the site of a lighthouse, semaphore station, quarantine post, customs control point, and a home for retired naval officers. It is now used as an inspection station by the Turkish Navy; the present quaint structure dates from the eighteenth century, and is one of the most distinctive landmarks on the lower Bosphorus.

The summit of the low hill behind Şemsi Paşa Camii is surmounted by Rum Mehmet Paşa Camii, the oldest mosque in Üsküdar, erected in 1471. Mehmet Paşa was a Byzantine Greek

ÜSKÜDAR

The Guz-Couli, or Maiden's Tower

Kız Kulesi

(in Turkish, *Rum*) who converted to Islam after the Conquest and became one of Fatih's vezirs. This is the most Byzantine in appearance of the early Ottoman mosques in Istanbul. Its most distinctively Byzantine features are the high cylindrical drum of the dome, the external cornice following the curve of the high-arched windows, and the square dome base broken by the projection of the great dome arches. The prayer-room is covered by the central dome, which has smooth pendentives, and a semidome over the *kıble* end, with chambers on either side completely cut off from the central area. The founder's *türbe* stands in the graveyard behind the mosque.

A winding street leads southward from Rum Mehmet Paşa Camii around the Salacak promontory, an area that is believed to be the site of the Byzantine palace of Scutarion. Near the southern end of the street we come to the imposing baroque mosque known as Ayazma Camii, which takes its name from the holy well on its site. The mosque was built in 1757-60 for Mustafa III, who dedicated to his mother, the Valide Sultan Mihrişah Emine. It is one of the more successful of the baroque mosques, especially on the exterior. A handsome entrance portal opens on to a courtyard from which a pretty flight of semicircular steps leads up to the mosque porch; on the left is a large cistern whose waters flow from the *ayazma* for which the mosque is named; beyond that an elaborate two-storied colonnade gives access to the imperial loge. The upper structure is also diversified with little domes and turrets, and numerous windows give light to the interior. The interior, as in many baroque mosques, is less successful, though the gray marble gallery along the entrance wall, supported by slender columns, is effective. Behind the mosque there is a picturesque graveyard with some interesting old tombstones.

Leaving by the south gate and following the street to the west, we come to Doğancılar Caddesi, the Avenue of the Falconers. At the corner there are two pretty fountains in the baroque style, both dating from the eighteenth century. Turning right here, we come at the end of the street to a *türbe* of the classical Ottoman period.

ÜSKÜDAR

Constantinople from Scutari

View from the Ferry at Scutari

This severely plain tomb was built by Sinan for Hacı Mehmet Paşa, who died in 1559. It stands on an octagonal terrace bristling with tombstones and overshadowed by a dying terebinth tree.

The wide street just ahead leads downhill past a little park. The third turning on the right followed by the first on the left leads to an elaborate and delightful *külliye*, the Ahmediye mosque and *medrese*. Built in 1722 by Eminzade Hacı Emin Zade, Comptroller of the Arsenal under Ahmet III, it is perhaps Istanbul's last baroque building complex in the classical style, though verging towards the baroque. Roughly square in layout, it has the porticoes and cells of the *medrese* along two sides; the library, one entrance portal and the mosque occupy a third side, while the fourth has the main gate complex with the *dershane* above and a graveyard alongside. The whole plan is, however, very irregular because of the alignment of the surrounding streets and the slope of the ground. The dome of the little mosque is supported by scallop-shell squinches and has a finely carved *mimber* and *Kuran kürsüsü*. The library and the *dershane* over the two gates are the two most attractive features and show great ingenuity of design.

At the southwest corner of the courtyard a stairway under the *dershane* leads to the street below. A short narrow lane opposite the outer gate leads to Toptaşı Caddesi, the Avenue of the Cannon Ball. We turn right here and follow the avenue for about 600 meters, as it leads up into the hills above lower Üsküdar, with fleeting views of the Bosphorus down below. Toward the top of the hill we turn left on Valide İmareti Sokağı, which brings us to Atik Valide Camii, the great mosque complex that dominates upper Üsküdar.

The mosque complex of Atik Valide was built by Sinan in 1583 for the Valide Sultan Nur Banu, wife of Selim II and mother of Murat III. This is the most splendid and extensive of all Sinan's constructions in Istanbul, with the single exception of the Süleymaniye. Besides the mosque itself, the *külliye* consists of a *medrese*, a hospital, a school for reading the Kuran, a *hamam*, an *imaret* and a caravansarai, where visiting merchants were put up

ÜSKÜDAR 153

free for three days. All these buildings are still in existence and most are in good condition, though several form part of a prison and cannot be visited. Altogether this is certainly one of the half-dozen most impressive monuments of Ottoman architecture in the whole of Turkey.

An alley beside the graveyard brings us to the *avlu*, or courtyard of Atik Valide Camii. This is one of the most beautiful of all the mosque courtyards in the city, a grandly proportioned cloister with domed porticoes supported on marble columns; in the center is the *şadırvan*, or ablution fountain, surrounded by many ancient plane trees and cypresses.

The mosque is entered through an elaborate double porch, the outer one with a penthouse roof, the inner domed and with elegant tiled inscriptions over the windows. Inside we find a wide rectangular room with a central dome supported by a hexagonal arrangement of pillars and columns; to north and south are side aisles each with two domed bays; the aisles were added at a late date, and although on a close examination the arrangement leads to certain anomalies, the general impression is very attractive. There are galleries around three sides of the room, and the wooden ceilings under some of them preserve that rich painting typical of the period: floral and arabesque designs in black, red and gold. The *mihrap* is in a square projecting apse entirely revetted in magnificent Iznik tiles of the best period. Also notable are the window-frames of deep red conglomerate marble with shutters richly inlaid with mother-of-pearl. The *mihrap* and *mimber* are fine works in carved marble.

The *medrese* of the complex stands at a lower level than the mosque, and is entered by a staircase in the west wall of the courtyard. Its own courtyard is almost as pretty as that of the mosque itself and is oddly irregular, having five domed bays to the north but only three to the south. The *dershane* is in the center of the west side in the axis of the mosque though at an obtuse angle to it, and it projects over the street below, forming an archway. Leaving the *medrese* by the gate in the south side, we walk around the building and pass under this picturesque archway. At the next corner beyond it stands the large hospital of the *külliye*, also highly irregular in plan but quite as attractive as the other buildings. These various irregularities are partly due to the alignment of the surrounding streets and to the varying level of the terrain. It is possible, however, that they were courted by Sinan to give variety and liveliness to his design, for he could have avoided them had he so chosen.

The other buildings of the *külliye* are either part of the prison or in a half ruined condition. The double *hamam* has lost its two entrance chambers and the rest is used as a carpentry shop, while the caravansarai is partly incorporated into the prison, partly used as a storehouse. It is to be hoped that the prison will be relocated and that this interesting and important complex will be restored to its original condition.

Nur Banu was one of the most important women in the history of Topkapı Sarayı. During the reign of Selim I she was Birinci Kadın, or First Wife, since she was the mother of the heir apparent, the future Murat III. She was the power behind the throne, beginning a period of Ottoman history known as the "Rule of Women," for the Sultan, known to the Turks as Selim the Sot, totally neglected affairs of state and spent his time drinking and enjoying the company of his women in the Harem. As Evliya Çelebi wrote of Selim: "He was an amiable monarch, took much delight in the conversations of poets and learned men, and indulged in wine and gaiety. He was a sweet-natured sovereign, but much given to women and wine." Selim died in the evening of 21 December 1574 at the age of fifty-four, after having fallen in his bath while in a drunken stupor. On the night of his death Nur Banu had her slaves murder five of the six young royal princes, all of them sons of other women, so that her own son Murat would succeed to the throne without opposition. Nur Banu thus became Valide Sultan, and to solidify her power she corrupted her son Murat III by supplying him with hordes of beautiful young women for his Harem, where he spent most of his reign, fathering 103

ÜSKÜDAR 155

children, according to the official register of the Saray, a record for the Ottoman dynasty.

We leave the *külliye* via Çinili Cami Sokağı, the continuation of Valide İmareti Sokağı. After a walk of about a kilometer this brings us to Çinili Cami, the Tiled Mosque. This small *külliye* was built in 1640 by the Valide Sultan Kösem, wife of Ahmet I and mother of Sultans Murat IV and İbrahim. The mosque, surrounded by a pretty garden filled with flowers and trees, is small and simple, just a square room covered by a dome. The mosque is decorated on the facade and in the interior by a revetment of Iznik tiles; these date from just after the best period but they are still quite fine, chiefly pale blue and turquoise on a white ground. The *mimber* of white marble has its own carving elegantly picked out in gold, red and green, with a tiled conical roof. The porch of the mosque is a baroque addition, as is the minaret, of which the *şerefe* has a corbel of very pretty folded-back acanthus leaves, unique in the city. In the courtyard there is a very fine *şadırvan* with a huge witch's cap for a roof, and a tiny *medrese*, triangular in shape, sloping headlong downhill. Just outside the precinct wall is a handsome primary school, and not far off there is a large *hamam*, both of which are part of Kösem's *külliye*.

Kösem was the last of the really powerful women in the history of Topkapı Sarayı. Her name was originally Anastasia, the daughter of a Greek priest on the Aegean island of Tinos, where she was captured by Turkish pirates and sold to the Harem in Topkapı Sarayı. There she was given the name Kösem and became a concubine of the future Ahmet I, bearing him two sons, Murat and İbrahim. When Ahmet I became Sultan in 1603 she assumed the position of First Wife, but with his untimely death fourteen years later Kösem was banished to the Old Saray on the Third Hill, where she remained through the reigns of Mustafa I (1617-18, 1622-23) and Osman II (1618-22), both of whom were assassinated by the Janissaries. Then in 1623 Kösem's eldest son succeeded to the throne as Murat IV, whereupon she triumphantly returned to Topkapı Sarayı. After the death of Murat in 1640 her second son, known to the Turks as Crazy İbrahim, succeeded as Sultan, whereupon Kösem continued as Valide Sultan throughout his reign, which ended when he was executed in 1648. Kösem continued to dominate the Harem during the early years of the reign of İbrahim's son and successor Mehmet IV, who was only five years old when he became Sultan. But Mehmet's mother, Turhan Hatice, eventually asserted her power as the rightful Valide Sultan, and one night in 1654 she had the Chief Black Eunuch strangle Kösem. Turhan Hatice herself never exerted significant power, and so with Kösem's death came the effective end of the "Rule of Women," which historians consider to be one of the major factors in the decline of the Ottoman Empire.

There are two places of interest to see on the southern side of Üsküdar, just north of Kadıköy on the Marmara. These are the Selimiye barracks and the Crimean War Cemetery, both of which are most easily approached by going south along the shore road in Üsküdar as far as the *iskele* at Harem, turning inland on Selimiye İskele Caddesi.

This brings us to the Selimiye barracks, the enormous four-towered structure that forms the most prominent landmark on the Asian coast at the mouth of the Bosphorus.

The original barracks here were wooden structures erected by Selim III in 1799 to house the men of his New Army, the modern force with which he hoped to replace the Janissaries. But these barracks burned down in 1808, shortly after Selim was deposed and then killed by the Janissaries. New stone barracks were erected on the same site by Mahmut II in 1828, two years after he finally destroyed the Janissaries. This building had only a single wing, with the other three added by Sultan Abdülmecit in the years 1842-53. The four enormous wings have three stories surrounding a vast quadrangular parade ground; at the corners there are five-storeyed towers with tall turrets above. During the Crimean War the barracks served as a British military hospital, along with the barracks at Kuleli on the Bosphorus, both of which were under the direction of Florence Nightingale in 1855-56. After the war the Selimiye barracks was once again used to house Turkish soldiers, as they still do today. Florence Nightingale's quarters in the northeast tower have been restored as they were in 1855-56, and they are open to the public as a museum.

Opposite the main entrance to the barracks is the Selimiye Camii, the mosque that Selim III built for the soldiers of his New Army. Erected in 1803-04, it is the last of the baroque mosques in Istanbul and one of the most handsome. Not only are its proportions and details most attractive, but it is situated in a lovely garden shaded by three ancient plane trees. The interior of the mosque is somewhat stark, though of impressive proportions. The western gallery, the *mihrap* and the *mimber* are all of highly polished gray marble, giving the interior of this seldom visited mosque a unique though sombre charm.

The huge building to the south of the Selimiye barracks is the Haydarpaşa Lisesi, behind which we find the exceptionally well-maintained Crimean War Cemetery. Many of the graves here are those of British soldiers and nurses who died in the nearby Selimiye barracks during the Crimean War. Also buried here are British and Commonwealth soldiers who died in Istanbul after suffering wounds at Gallipoli and in other campaigns in the Middle East and the Caucasus during World War I, along with members of the British community in Istanbul, whose graves date back to the first half of the nineteenth century.

The oldest and largest Turkish cemetery in Istanbul is the Karacaahmet Mezarlığı, which is in the hills above Üsküdar northeast of the Selimiye barracks and the Haydarpaşa Lisesi. According to tradition, the cemetery is named after Karacaahmet, a sainted Turkish warrior who was killed here in the mid-fourteenth century when the Ottoman army conquered Chrysopolis and Chalcedon; however the oldest known tombstone dates only to 1521. As so often happens, Karaca Ahmet's grave was miraculously discovered in later times, revealed to a dervish in a dream. A *türbe* was then erected to enshrine the saint's remains, along with a *tekke* to house the dervishes who looked after it. The original *türbe* was replaced by the present tomb in the nineteenth century, while the *tekke* was demolished in the early years of the Republic. After the conquest of Constantinople in 1453 many Turks chose to be buried here rather than in the cemeteries on the European side of the city, since the Karacaahmet burial ground is in Asia, nearer the sacred city of Mecca. Evliya Çelebi lists a number of "great Sheikh and Saints" who chose to be buried in the Karacaahmet cemetery, the most notable being his spiritual mentor.

Among those buried near the *tekke* of Karaca Ahmet is Asumani Dede, a man lost in contemplation, who lifted his eyes always to heaven, and talked to himself. When Selim I marched into Persia he encouraged him, foretelling the Sultan's victory at the battle of Chaldiran. Near him is buried the famous Sheikh Hedayi Mehmet, who died in 1628. One night he had a vision of hell, which so frightened him that as soon as he awoke he gave away all that he possessed and set himself up as a Sheikh on his carpet in Scutari. In short he kissed the hands of seven Emperors and marched by the stirrup of Sultan Ahmet I. He had a hundred and seventy disciples, and was the pole-star of his time, the treasurer of mystic truth, the fountain of knowledge, and the candle of the *mihrap* of contemplation. His excellent qualities and good works exceed all number. He composed no less than a hundred volumes filled with spiritual songs on ascetic subjects. Praise be to God that I, poor Evliya, had the good fortune to converse with him; he covered me with his cloak, and adopted me as his spiritual child. I glorify myself that I have heard an infinite number of good maxims from his mouth, and that I have kissed his blessed hand.

The cemetery of Karacaahmet is a place of haunting beauty and serenity, with acre after acre of serried but topsy-turvy tombstones lying in the dappled shade of groves of spectral cypresses, the only sounds those of bird song and the sighing of the occasional breeze in the treetops. Many of the older tombstones are beautifully sculptured and inscribed, crowned with representations of the deceased, from which we learn their sex and station. The older tombstones of the men are surmounted with a turban, which

ÜSKÜDAR

was banned after 1826, to be replaced by the fez, which tops the funerary stones of the later Ottomans, till it too was banned in the early years of the Republic. Among the turbaned tombstones we see here and there the headdress of a Grand Vezir, a Pasha, an Ağa of the Janissaries, a Sipahi, a Chief Black Eunuch, a dervish Sheikh. Those of the women are decorated with floral designs in low relief and adorned with archaic headdresses reminiscent of the Arabian Nights, sometimes draped in a shawl, the face of the stone carved with floral designs in relief, with the number of roses symbolizing the number of her children, the turban of a princess emblazoned with stars, that of a Valide Sultan encircled with a tiara. The faces of the tombstones also have calligraphic inscriptions recording the dates of birth and death of the deceased, often with a witty epitaph in which they bid farewell to the mortal world. A number of these humorous epitaphs were translated for the present author in 1961 by Cevat Şakir Kabaağaçlı, the departed Turkish writer better known as the Fisherman of Halicarnassus, who wrote of them in an essay called *Laughing Tombstones:*

'A pity to good-hearted İsmail Efendi, whose death caused great sadness among his friends. Having caught the illness of love at the age of seventy, he took the bits between his teeth and dashed full gallop to paradise.'

'Stopping his ears with his fingers, Judge Mehmet hied off from this beautiful world, leaving his wife's cackling and his mother-in-law's gabbling.'

(On a wayside tomb): 'Oh passerby, spare me your prayers, but please don't steal my tombstone!'

'I could have died as well without a doctor than with the quack that friends set upon me.'

'I have swerved away from you a long time. But in soil, air, cloud, rain, plant, flower, butterfly or bird, I am always with you.'

(On a tombstone with the relief of three trees, an almond, a cypress and a peach-tree, peaches being the symbols of a woman's breasts): 'I've planted these trees so that people might know my fate. I loved an almond-eyed, cypress-tall maiden, and bade farewell to this beautiful world without savoring her peaches.'

A very popular excursion from Üsküdar is to Büyük Çamlıca, the Great Pine Mountain, the highest peak of Mount Bulgurlu, 262 meters above sea level. The pine-clad peak of Büyük Çamlıca is about five kilometers east of İskele Meydanı, approached by the main highway leading inland from the Bosphorus. The Turkish Touring and Automobile Club has now created a park on the summit of the hill, along with a café and an old-fashioned teahouse, so that it is a very pleasant place to spend an afternoon. The view from the western belvedere is magnificent, including the whole of the lower Bosphorus from the Narrows to the Sea of Marmara, with the cupolas and spires of the old city of Stamboul silhouetted on the ridge of the Constantinopolitan peninsula above the Golden Horn, the great dome of Haghia Sophia hovering over the pavilions and gardens of Topkapı Sarayı on the ancient acropolis of Byzantium. From the eastern side of the summit one can see the Princes Isles floating serenely in the pale blue mirror of the Marmara, and sometimes on the clearest of halcyon days in midwinter there is a distant view of the snow-capped and cloud-plumed peak of Uludağ, the Great Mountain, known in antiquity as Mount Olympus of Bithynia. Miss Pardoe devotes one of the essays in *The Beauties of the Bosphorus* to the "View from Mount Bulgurlhu," and the accompanying print by Charles Bartlett, entitled "Constantinople from Scutari," shows that the panorama is the one seen from Büyük Çamlıca; as she writes:

The scene which is spread out before the wanderer, as he stands upon the dusky mountain of Bulgurlhu, with the town of Scutari immediately at his feet, and the city of Constantinople in its frame of clear and pellucid water, is the one which throughout his after life, be of what duration it may be, he can never cease to remember. He looks down into the mysterious gardens of Serai Bournou, far out over the glittering Propontis, along the shores of the Bosphorus, into the Golden Horn, upon 'St. Sophia's gleaming dome'; on the seven hills of the imperial city, the gloomy remains of the Seven Towers, the ancient walls of Byzantium, the modern palaces of the Sultans, the fair islands of the Sea of Marmara, and the far-off and snow-crested Mount Olympus, lording it over the fertile plains of Broussa.... This is, perhaps, the most favorable point for contemplating Stamboul in all its extent, and fully comprehending its extraordinary magnificence as a whole; its singular outline, its ocean girdle, where the blue waves seem to follow lovingly whithersoever the sinuousities of the shores invite them; its thousand domes and its shaft-like minarets beckoning to the blue heavens, against which they glitter like polished ivory... its cypress groves stretching down to the water's edge; and all the blended beauties of the unrivalled locality.

Miss Pardoe's reference to Haghia Sophia is a paraphrased quote from Canto V of Byron's *Don Juan,* written after he saw the view from the Great Çamlıca during his visit to Istanbul in 1810:

> The European with the Asian shore
> Sprinkled with palaces; the Ocean stream
> Here and there studded with a seventy-four;
> Sophia's cupola with a golden gleam;
> The twelve isles, and the more I could dream,
> Far less describe, present the very view
> Which charm'd the charming Mary Montagu.

Byron here refers to Lady Mary Wortley Montagu's description of the Bosphorean scene, written in one of her letters from Istanbul in the years 1716-18:

The pleasure of going in a barge to Chelsea is not comparable to that of rowing on the canal of the sea here where, for twenty miles together down the Bosphorus, the most beautiful variety of prospects present themselves. The Asian side is covered with fruit trees, villages, and the most delightful landscapes in nature; on the European stands Constantinople, situated on seven hills, showing an agreeable mixture of gardens, pines and cypress trees, palaces, mosques and public buildings, raised one above the other, with as much beauty and appearance of symmetry as you ever saw....

Evliya Çelebi often strolled among these hills, and he lists half-a-dozen of his favorite walks on the heights above the Asian end of the Bosphorus; as he writes:

Scutari is surrounded on all sides with delightful walks, the finest of which, however, are those of the imperial gardens. The most celebrated of all is that of Büyük Çamlıca, where a kiosk was built by the present monarch, Murat IV, the chronograph of which was composed by me, poor Evliya.

Evliya's lines take us back more than three centuries, but we can go back more than eleven centuries before that for the earliest description of the view from this mountain above the lower end of the Bosphorus on its Asian shore. Thus was written by Procopius, court chronicler of Justinian and the author of a multi-volumed history of the Emperor's wars. At the Emperor's request, Procopius wrote an account of the buildings that Justinian had erected in Constantinople and elsewhere in his vast empire, a work that he completed c. 555. Procopius begins this work, entitled Edifices, with a study of the topography of Constantinople, starting with a description of the city as seen from the heights across the strait. As he writes: "The city is surrounded by a garland of waters...," by which he meant the Sea of Marmara, the Golden Horn and the Bosphorus, which still divide and define the ancient imperial city standing astride the strait between Europe and Asia. Such is the view from the heights above Üsküdar, the ancient City of Gold.

CHAPTER TEN
A CAFE ON THE BOSPHORUS

The Bosphorean scene has changed greatly since the present author first arrived in Istanbul in early September of 1960, though some essential things remain the same, perhaps because they are part of a continuing dream. The dream would have begun when he sat down in Nazmi's café in Bebek and spent an autumnal afternoon looking out on the Bosphorus, observing its passing maritime life, its changing colors as the sun set behind the European hills and reflected its golden fire in the windows of the *yalıs* across the way in Asia, where the full moon then rose to cast its ashen light over the water in the lambent beam that the Turks call *mehtap*. The years did indeed pass like a dream when one remembers them from the point of view of a seat in Nazmi's, where Rıza Kaptan and Captain Abi, as we called him, and all of the other fishermen of Bebek stored their gear and passed their hours when they were not fishing on the Bosphorus. Some of the Bosphorean lore that we learned from Captain Abi and the other fishermen of Bebek appeared in *Stamboul Sketches,* a book that the present author published in 1974, in a chapter entitled "A Café on the Bosphorus." The chapter was actually a eulogy for Nazmi's, which closed one autumn day in 1972, never to reopen, its site now buried under the Venüs Apartmanı, though those of us who remember it still feel a tug on our heart as we pass it by walking along the quay.

And so this final chapter now slips back into this old dream by simply repeating without change the description of the Bosphorean scene as it appeared in "A Café on the Bosphorus," hoping thus to evoke a way of life that has now all but vanished in Istanbul.

***

A CAFE ON THE BOSPHORUS

Everyone has their favorite spot for Bosphorus-watching; our own is Nazmi's, a venerable waterfront cafe near the village of Bebek. For more than half a century Nazmi's has been a gathering-place for the local fishermen and students and for the intellectuals and would-be intellectuals of Stamboul, especially those whose thought and talk require the stimulation provided by cognac and *rakı* in a seaside setting. And if the talk of philosophy, art and politics becomes too intense at times, and if the rival political factions sometimes shatter Nazmi's windows and splinter his chairs upon one another's heads in their drunken debates, pay them no heed, but fill your glass again, while the rising moon silvers the placid waters of Bebek Bay.

Some prefer to sit in Nazmi's by day, for then the students and intellectuals are abed, and one can enjoy the view undisturbed by their violent discussions. One will then meet the fishermen and boatmen of Bebek, who store their gear in Nazmi's back room and who sit and drink there in their off hours, which are numerous, judging from the perpetual insobriety of these salt-encrusted old characters. And so to Nazmi's back room we will go, to learn some of the maritime lore of the Bosphorus. If you sit and drink there with old Captain Abi he will point out to you some of the picturesque boats that sail along the Bosphorus, lineal descendants of the craft that have plied these straits since the days of Jason and the Argonauts: the *taka*, workhorse of the Bosphorus, broad of beam, peaked bow and high fantail, lumbering beauties painted in all the brightest colors of the sun's spectrum; the *mavna*, single-masted craft with lateen rig and raking stern; the *salapurya*, cousin to the *mavna* but smaller and more snub-nosed; the *bombarda*, the old-fashioned caique from the Aegean isles, often seen loaded to the gunwales with wine from the Marmara; the *martika*, the sturdy two-masted Black Sea coaster; the *karavela*, or caravel, now almost extinct, the last examples of those ships in which Columbus sailed; the *gagalı*, another ancient craft, of which only one or two still remain, high poop-deck and transomed stern, bow shaped like the curve of a parrot's beak and decorated with the sign of the oculus, or talismanic eye, by which sailors have warded off the

A CAFE ON THE BOSPHORUS 165

evils of the deep since the days of the ancient Egyptians. Captain Abi will also point out to you with pride the boats in which the Bosphorus fishermen make their living. The most beautiful of these are the rowing *kayık*s, long, slim, swift craft, each manned by about a dozen oarsmen. These *kayık*s are towed in line behind powerful *mavna*s, ready to dart out across the water like sea swallows when a school of fish is sighted by the lookout, who is pinioned like a sailor-Christ on his cross-like perch atop the lead boat.

But if Nazmi's back room is empty you should know that the *lüfer*, or bluefish, are running and that Captain Abi, together with every other fisherman on the Bosphorus, is out in his *sandal*, or rowboat, and he will not return to the café until he has caught enough to support his family for the season and to ensure his winter supply of *rakı*. The *lüfer* fishing-fleet represents one of the most picturesque spectacles on the Bosphorus; each *sandal* equipped with a brilliant lamp shining down into the depths to attract the dazzled fish, together looking like a swarm of marine fireflies drifting down the dark blue stream, the night sky a lighter blue above them, crowded in luminous clusters down all the bays and coves of the Bosphorus, individual lights flitting back and forth between the invisible continents. One evening as I sat watching this extraordinary display, this yearly recurring festival of the marine lamps which is one of the delights of our life on the Bosphorus, one of the lights detached itself from the others and headed towards the quay where I was sitting. Soon I could see that it was an old fisherman who was rowing powerfully to shore to meet his old wife, who had come down to the quay with his pailful of dinner. They conversed briefly in the yellow light of the boat-lamp and then the fisherman bade his wife goodnight and rowed back out again into the dark blue stream, clouds of white sea birds screaming around him. Soon his light had joined the others out on the Bosphorus and they drifted slowly down the strait. Then I walked slowly back along the quay to Nazmi's, to sit there alone and watch through the night these marine galaxies, rivaling the stars in their beauty and luminosity.

When the decimated *lüfer*-school finally completes its slow

166   A CAFE ON THE BOSPHORUS

annual transit of the straits, the fishermen return to their cafés and teahouses along the Bosphorus. You might then sit yourself by the fire in Nazmi's back room and learn from Captain Abi some of the lore of the wondrous winds and storms that trouble the straits and keep the fishermen happily idle through most of the year. That fierce wind now howling outside of Nazmi's, dashing salt spray on the windows and whistling through the cracks in the walls, is Karayel, the Black Wind, blowing from the cold northeastern quarter of the compass. Later in the winter you will feel the lash of Yıldız, the Star-Wind, as it shrieks in from due north and flays any fisherman foolhardy enough to be out of doors in that icy season. Then in January you will feel the wrath of Poyraz, the northwest wind named after King Boreas, mythical ruler of the obstreperous airs. Poyraz howls down the strait from the frigid Black Sea and whitens with snow the hillsides of the Bosphorus, lays white shrouds on the columnar cypresses, powders the leaden domes of village mosques, the roofs of *yalıs* and seaside palaces, the crenellated towers and battlements of the Castles of Europe and Asia, and tints the teal-blue waters of the Bosphorus with the milk-white reflections of scudding snow-clouds. In February the wind suddenly shifts to the southeast and Keşişleme, the Wind of Mount Olympus, begins to blow moistly and the dismal winter rains begin. Cold rain pours down from lowering gray clouds for weeks on end, soaking our overcoats, filling our shoes, dripping from our beards, fogging our spectacles and our minds, drowning the town in filthy mud and discoloring the Bosphorus in ugly brown streaks. We swear then to sail away from this dark and cheerless, cloud-shrouded town and never again return, for it is doomed to a watery death and we are too, if we remain. But Captain Abi, ordering another *rakı* at our expense, counsels us to be of good cheer. This alcoholic almanac then acquaints us with the windy signs and portents of approaching spring and good weather. The worst of winter is done, he says, when you feel the fresh zephyr called Hüzün Fırtınası, the Agreeable Storm, which wafts in across

A CAFE ON THE BOSPHORUS 167

the Marmara in early March. This harbinger is soon followed by another, Kozkavuran Fırtınası, the Storm of Roasting Walnuts, which blows across the Bosphorus from the greening hills of Anatolia. Then in rapid succession you will see perennial vernal signs and feel the seasonal winds that accompany them. The returning birds: Çaylak Fırtınası, the Storm of the Kites; Karakuş Fırtınası, the Storm of the Blackbirds; Kırlangıç Fırtınası, the Storm of the Swallows; Kuğu Fırtınası, the Storm of the Swans; Kukulya Fırtınası, the Storm of the Cuckoos. Signs floral: Filizkıran Fırtınası, the Storm of Green Buds; Çiçek Fırtınası, the Storm of Flowers; Kabak Meltemi, the Squash Breeze. Signs celestial: Ülker Fırtınası, the Storm of the Pleiades; Gündönümü Fırtınası, the Storm of the Summer Solstice. Then one day you will look out of Nazmi's window and see a long stately line of storks soaring across the Bosphorus from Asia in their annual return to their ancestral nests in the cemetery of Eyüp above the Golden Horn. Now the Bosphorus becomes azure blue again, flowering judases purple the hillsides and then mature into a virginal green, giant *çınar*s spread their dappled shade over Nazmi's courtyard and flowering vines carpet the café pavement with blossoms. And so spring greets the local fishermen, now staggering out from Nazmi's back room, their eyes bleary from the smoke and drink of a long winter. In this season you may be troubled by the cruel beauty of nightingale-song when you stagger home by moonlight from a late party, and in your bittersweet melancholy decide that you will sleep out in the old dervish graveyard under the walls of Rumelihisarı. You will be awakened there by the throbbing sounds of *taka*s and *mavna*s laboring up the strait and feel the warmth of the sun newly risen out of Asia. You arise then and walk back to Nazmi's for a therapeutic beer and find the cobbled quay deep in brilliant blue and green and scarlet fish-nets spread out to dry in the sun. Laz fishermen and their families sit on the cobbles amid these gorgeous billows of twine and patiently mend their nets, while a handsome idiot youth plays haunting melodies on a bagpipe to ease the monotony of their work. His primitive music seems to call out from their winter quarters all of the camp followers of good weather. Soon the quay is crowded with street-boys from town, who spread out their ragged clothes to air on the cobbles while they dive and splash through the rapidly flowing garbage generated by the crowds of corpulent diners gluttonizing in the waterfront restaurants. Sellers of sweet corn set up their smoking engines on the quay and vie for the penny trade of the passers-by with peddlers of sweets, pastries, ice cream and fishing gear. The *saz* player returning exhausted to his bed from the dives of Beyoğlu passes on the quay his friend, the balloon-seller, who left the same bed an hour before. Villainous-looking Gypsies lead bears and pound tambourines, on the lookout for larceny, while across the road their wives beg with their infants at their breasts, looking like fallen Madonnas, while their dark-visaged mothers traffic in flowers, herbs, berries and mushrooms, or whatever else you might desire on such a vernal day.

You might think that this fine weather would move Captain Abi and his friends from their firm seats in Nazmi's and induce them to do some fishing in the Bosphorus; but no, they find it more profitable to rent out their sandals to amateur fishermen in the summer. They, the professionals, can then pocket the amateur's cash and laugh at his ineffectual attempts to catch their fish, while they swill *rakı* and enjoy their *keyif* throughout the summer undisturbed by work. Then, if you are prepared to endow him with a few more *rakı*s, Captain Abi will identify for you the sweet breezes that ruffle the wisteria vines in the café, fill the sails of boats skimming across Bebek Bay, and propel the fleecy clouds that soar across the cerulean sky. These fair winds, Captain Abi says, will follow in turn on their appointed days: Çarkdönümü Fırtınası, the Storm of the Turning Windmills; Kara Erik and Kızıl Erik Fırtınası, the Storms of Black and Red Plums; and Kestane Harası Fırtınası, the Storm of Ripening Chestnuts. But then there may be days when you find Captain Abi cross and uncommunicative, and you should know that the evil wind Lodos is blowing from the southwest, filling the Bosphorus with stinking garbage and the sinus with black phlegm, shrouding the city with a miasmatic haze and transforming it into an airless, sweating, seething, quarreling Levantine hell. But never mind, for the Melteme will soon come, sweeping in from the Marmara to dispel all foul airs and bad feelings. Captain Abi will soon become his old affable self once again and may even buy you a *rakı*, while he catalogues for you the winds of late summer and early fall, the most glorious season of all along the Bosphorus. These blow in turn as the *çınar*s turn gold over Nazmi's courtyard and the grapes ripen on the trellis over your head; Turna Geçimi Fırtınası, the Storm of the Passing Cranes; Meryem Ana Fırtınası, the Storm of Mother Mary; Bağ Bozumu Fırtınası, the Storm of the Vintage; and Koç Katımı Fırtınası, the Storm of the Mating Ram. Then the skies above the Bosphorus begin to darken once again, harsh winds blow down the strait from the north, and Captain Abi and his friends begin to move out of their seats in Nazmi's - it is time to get their *sandal*s ready and to work again, the fish will soon be running. You will know when the *çiroz* are back when you see these little silver fish in their tens of thousands hung out to dry from every clothes-line along the Bosphorus. When the *levrek* are running, Captain Abi and his mates will set out their nets from the *dalyan* in Bebek Bay, and then when they are full, haul them in until the quay is deep in thrashing, gasping, gleaming fish, and the cobbles are covered with scales and slippery with gore. And when the word spreads that a school of *istavrit* are swimming down the strait - beware! For then every man, woman and child in town will rush to Bebek with their hooks and lines. They stand ten deep on the quay, casting their lines wildly into the water, impaling one another with their hooks, their weights crashing through the windows of passing buses, fouling their lines in the propellers of the ferries crossing Bebek Bay, then all dashing into taxis and leaving suddenly when the rumor spreads that the *istavrit* school has swum on to Arnavutköy.

With the streets of our village redolent with the savory odor of frying fish and the cats grown corpulent on fish heads and other leavings, then we can all face winter cheerfully. In that mellow autumnal mood we sit under the falling leaves in Nazmi's courtyard, sipping our *rakı* to keep warm and reminiscing over the twice-picked bones of our *barbunya*, wondering if we will ever have the will to leave this beautiful but ruinous town. Then we look out along the Bosphorus and watch the blue *mavna*s and their trailing company of *kayık*s as they set out to catch *kılıç balığı*, the swordfish, far out on the Marmara. We see them again when they return in early evening, and hear the fisherman's flute as he plays for his tipsy shipmates dancing on the fantail of the *mavna*. But all of these great fishing days begin, as Captain Abi will tell you, only after that late October squall called Balık Fırtınası, the Storm of Fish.

And so the year passes in our village, a cycle of seasons and their ever-recurring winds, and so we pass our idle hours and days, seated in a café beside the Bosphorus.

***

The years pass and the scene changes, but at its core something eternal remains the same, as if this place had an immortal soul, as the Bosphorus continues to surge powerfully between the continents in its unending flow, streaming like time's river in the country of dreams.

INDEX

A

Abaza 28
Abbas Hilmi Paşa 115
Abdülaziz (1861-76) 27, 38, 42, 48, 72, 138
Abdülhamit I (1774-89) 32, 47, 85, 136
Abdülhamit II (1876- 1909) 29, 37, 44, 45, 67, 68, 72, 78, 80, 83, 138
Abdullah Paşa 74
Abdülmecit (1839-61) 34, 37, 38, 41, 44, 47, 72, 112, 126, 156
Abu Sufyan 15
Acar Burnu 108
Adam Czartoryski 112
Aelian 52
Agamemnon 32
Age of Tulips 41
Ahır (Stable) Köşkü 139
Ahmediye Camii 152
Ahmet Ağa Sokağı 71
Ahmet I (1603-17) 35, 155, 158
Ahmet III (1703-30) 41, 47, 144, 146, 152
Ahmet Paşa 111
Ahmet Vefik Paşa 67, 68
Aias 32
Ajantion 32, 33
Ajax 32
Akıntı Burnu 51, 52
Akoimetai 113
Akri Psomion 101
Alemdağ 122
Alexander the Great 29
Algiers 39, 40
Ali Paşa 19
Ali Pertek Camii 66
Alibey Suyu 5, 90
Altınkum 96
Amalfians 13
Amcazade Hüseyin Paşa Köprülü Yalısı 116
American College for Women 51
Amiri Wahibi 15
Ampelodes 102
Amycus 76, 109, 110
Anabasis 112
Anadolufeneri 2, 100
Anadolufeneri Burnu 102
Anadoluhisarı 1, 2, 62, 117, 119, 120, 123
Anadolukavağı 93, 94, 104, 105, 106, 107, 108
Anaplous 49
Anastasia 155
Andronicus I Comnenus (1183-85) 89

Ankara 10, 120
Apollo 9, 98
Apollonius 98, 109, 110
Apollonius of Rhodes 7, 97
Aquaducts: Eğrikemer 89; Güzelce Kemer 90; Maglova Kemeri 90; Uzunkemer 89
Arab 90
Arabia 24, 143
Archangel Michael 49, 76, 106
Areetes 105
Ares 106
Argo 7, 8, 97, 98, 99, 100, 101
Argonautica 7, 96, 98, 109
Argonauts 8, 11, 76, 93, 96, 97, 101, 110
Argos 33
Argyropolis 30, 32
Arifi Paşa Korusu 57
Arm of St. George 148
Armenia 27
Arnavutköy 51, 132
Artaxerxes II 113
Asian Cyanean Rock 102
Assyrian 88
Asumani Dede 158
Aşiyan 58
Aşiyan road 71
Atatürk, Kemal 10, 37, 38
Athamas of Boeotia 105
Athena 99, 100
Atik Valide Camii 152, 153
Ayazma Camii 150
Ayios (Saint) Mamas 39
Ayios Panteleon 140
Ayios Phocas 46, 76
Ayios Sideros 102
Ayios Yiorgios 79, 140
Ayvalık 85
Ayvasovski 38, 139
Azaryan Yalısı 86
Aziyade 130

B

Babylon 113
Baghdad 26
Baiazeth 120
Balta Oğlu (Son of the Axe) 72
Baltalimanı 72
Balyan, Kirkor 27, 34
Balyan, Nikogos 34, 37, 41, 47, 48, 126, 138
Balyan, Sarkis 108, 138

INDEX

Balyan Usta Yalısı 48
Barbarossa 39, 40
Barbyzes 89
Baron de Tott 96, 102
Bartlett, Charles 160
Bayram 27
Beşiktaş 38, 39, 41, 42
Bebek 51, 55, 58, 71, 72
Bebryces 76, 109, 110
Bed of Hercules 107
Bedouin 128
Beglier Bey 138
Belgrade Forest 88, 89
Belisarius 5
Benedictines 17
Beyazit I (1389-1403) 41, 62, 107, 120, 121
Beyazit II (1481-1512) 23, 24, 26, 111, 113
Beykoz 108, 109, 110, 111
Beykoz Çeşmesi 109
Beylerbeyi 1, 135, 136, 139
Beylerbeyi Camii 136
Beylerbeyi Sarayı 48, 135
Bezmiâlem Valide Sultan 34
Bithynia 112, 113
Bithynians 101
Black Virgin 18
Boğaziçi 11
Boğaziçi Köprüsü 48
Boğaziçi Üniversitesi 55
Bohemia 139
Boreas 96
Boulanger 38
Bridges: Boğaziçi Köprüsü 48; Fatih Sultan Mehmet Köprüsü 69, 72; Galata Köprüsü 11
Broussa 161
Buildings, castles: Black Stone 93; Castle of Hieron 94; Castle of the Incorporeal Saints 94; Castle of Yoros 104; Genoese Castle 104; Karataş 93
Buildings, churches: Archangel Michael 49, 76, 106; Ayios (Saint) Mamas 39; Ayios Panteleon 140; Ayios Phocas 46; Ayios Yiorgios 79, 140; Church of the Virgin 80; Haghia Sophia 160; Metanoia 133; Panayia 17,18; Repentance 133, 135; Spanish Chapel 86; St. Alexander 29, 113; St. Benoit 17; St. George 79; St. George of the Mangana 148; St. Gregory the Illuminator 17; St. John of Studius 113; St. John the Baptist 17; St. Nicholas 17; St. Sophia 160; St. Theodore of Tiron 84; Surp Kirkor Lusavoriç 17, 140; Tarabya Greek Orthodox church 82; Taxiarchs 51
Buildings, forts: Anadoluhisarı 1, 2, 62, 119, 120, 123; Baron de Tott's 102; Castle of Europe 128; Castle of Asia 123; Genoese fortress 91, 112; Güzelce 120; Gyropolis 96; Mavromoliotissa 94; Ottoman fort 98; Place of Vultures 96; Rumelihisarı 1, 2, 49, 55, 57, 71, 72, 106, 119, 120; Yoros 93, 105
Buildings, fountains: Beykoz Çeşmesi 109; Hekimoğlu Ali Paşa Çeşmesi 32; Küçüksu Çeşmesi 126, 128; Tophane Çeşmesi 23
Buildings, lighthouses: Anadolufeneri 2, 100; Rumelifeneri 2, 98, 100; Lightning 120
Buildings, kiosks: Ahır Köşkü 139; Beyaz Köşk 74; Çadır Köşkü 44, 78; Ihlamur Kasrı 41; Kalender Köşkü 80; Maiyet Köşkü 41; Malta Köşkü 44; Maslak Kasrı 78; Merasim Köşkü 41; Mermer Köşk 139; Sarı Köşk 139; Sepetçiler Kasrı 11, 13; Şale Köşkü 44, 45; Yeşil Sera 44
Buildings, mosques: Ahmediye Camii 152; Ali Pertek Camii 66; Atik Valide Camii 152, 153; Ayazma Camii 150; Beylerbeyi Camii 136; Cezayirli Gazi Hasan Paşa Camii 85; Cihangir Camii 28; Çinili Cami 155; Defterdar Camii 49; Dolmabahçe Camii 34, 47; Hacı Kemalettin 63; İskele Camii 144; İskender Paşa Camii 115, 116; Kaptan-ı Derya Cezayirli Gazi Hasan Paşa Camii 85; Kapudan Khalil Paşa Camii 79; Karabaş Mescidi 23; Kâtip Camii 57; Koca Defterdar Paşa Camii 85; Kuzguncuk Camii 140; Kılıç Ali Paşa Camii 23; Mecidiye Camii 44, 47; Mehmet Ağa 29; Molla Çelebi Camii 32; mosque in Anadoluhisarı 1; Nusretiye Camii 27, 34; Rum Mehmet Paşa Camii 148, 150; Selimiye Camii 157; Şemsi Paşa Camii 147, 148; Tophane Camii 27; Uryanizade Camii 140; Yeni Cami 13; Yeni Valide Camii 146; Yeraltı Camii 15
Buildings, museums: Deniz Müzesi 40; Kandilli Rasathanesi 132; Kasrı Hümayun 78; Resim ve Heykel Müzesi 41; Sadberk Hanım Museum 86
Buildings, palaces: Beylerbeyi Sarayı 48, 135, 138, 139; Çırağan Sarayı 42; Dolmabahçe Sarayı 35, 47, 126, 138, 139; Great Palace of Byzantium 6; Ihlamur Kasrı 41; Hidiv Kasrı 115; Küçük Esma Sultan Sarayı 47; Küçüksu Kasrı 126; Presidential Palace 80; Scutarion 150; Topkapı Sarayı 6, 13, 37, 146, 154, 155, 160; Yıldız Sarayı 43, 44, 139
Buildings, walls: Byzantine defence wall 13; Seven Towers 161; Theodosian walls 6, 84
Buildings, yalıs: Amcazade Hüseyin Paşa Köprülü Yalısı 116, 117; Azaryan Yalısı 86; Balyan Usta Yalısı 48; Ethem Pertev Yalısı 116; Hekimbaşı Salih Efendi Yalısı 116; Kıbrıslı Mustafa Emin Paşa Yalısı 128; Kırmızı (Red) Yalı 130; Sabancı mansion 76; Sadullah Paşa Yalısı 135; Şerifler Yalısı 74; Yılanlı Yalı 57, 58; Zaim Mustafa Paşa Yalısı 117
Bulgars 76
Burgaz 89
Büyük Çamlıca 4, 160, 162
Büyükdere 84, 85, 86, 89, 90
Büyükdere Limanı 84
Büyükliman 96
Byron 107, 118, 161
Byzantine defence wall 13
Byzantium 1, 6, 8, 9, 10, 11, 30

INDEX

Byzas 7, 9, 10

C

Calabria 19
Calais 96
Calpe 112, 113
Castle of Asia 123
Castle of Europe 128
Castle of Galata 15, 35
Castle of Hieron 94
Castle of the Incorporeal Saints 94
Castle of Yoros 104
Castor 110
Celaladin Rumi 42
Cemetaries: Şehitlik 68; Crimean War Cemetery 157; Evliyalar Tepesi 68; Hill of the Saints 68; Karacaahmet 158; Karacaahmet Mezarlığı 157; Kayalar 68, 71; Kayalar Mezarlığı 58; Place of Martyrs 68
Cenani Yalısı in Kanlıca 118
Cengiz Bektaş 139, 140
Cervantes 19
Cervantes, Miguel 19
Cevat Şakir Kabaağaçlı 159
Cezayirli Gazi Hasan Paşa Camii 85
Cezayirli Palabıyık 85
Chalcedon 9, 33, 94, 142
Chalkis 33
Charandas 33
China 139
Chryso Keras 5
Chrysokeramos 135
Chrysopolis 30, 142
Cicero 106
Cidaris 90
Cihangir 29
Cihangir Camii 28
Cities: Algiers 39, 40; Ankara 10, 120; Babylon 113; Bagdad 26; Broussa 161; Burgaz 89; Byzantium 30; Calabria 19; Çanakkale 88; Chalcedon 9, 33, 94; Chaldiran 158; City of Gold 30, 142, 162; City of Silver 30; Colchis 94; Cunaxa 113; Delphi 9; Erivan 74; Gallipol 85; İznik 88; Jerusalem 39; Kaffa 18; Kilyos 91; Kütahya 88; Lemnos 85; Lygos 9; Mecca 21, 32, 158; Medina 144; Megara 9, 33; Miletos 8; Paris 27; Pyrgos 89; Rethymnon 146; Rome 2, 10; Rum 2; Salamis 32; Samos 71; Sardis 113; Sinop 8; Sinope 8; *stinpoli* 6; Susa 70; Tinos 155; Tomi 91; Trebizond 79, 113; Tripoli 39; Troy 32; Tunis 20, 39, 40; Varna 91
Clashing Rocks 96, 97, 101
Colchis 94, 105, 106, 115
Column of Pompey 98
Comarodes 79
Comnenus, Manuel I. (1143-80) 94
Constantine the Great (324-37) 10, 49, 76

Constantine XI (1449-53) 60
Constantinople, Settings and Traits 58
Coracium 102
Cossacks 79, 83
Crete 146
Crimean War 55, 133
Crimean War Cemetery 157
Cunaxa 113
Cyanean Rocks 70, 97
Cybele 94
Cyrus the Younger 113
Czar Nicholas II 38
Czartoryski, Adam 112

Ç

Çadır Köşkü 44, 78
Çakal Limanı 102
Çamlıca 161, 162
Çanakkale 88
Çayırbaşı 85, 88
Çengelköy 135
Çinili Cami 155
Çinili Cami Sokağı 155
Çırağan Sarayı 42
Çubuklu 113, 115
Çubuklu Korusu 115

D

Dardanelles 3, 85
Darius 1, 69, 70, 71, 106
D'Aronco, Raimondo 45, 52
Defterdar Burnu 49
Defterdar Camii 49
Defterdar Paşa 49
Delphi 9
Deniz Müzesi 40
Denizcilik Bankası 15
Desenchantees 130
Dionysius Byzantius 52, 98, 110
Dios Sacra 102
Diplokion 39
Doğancılar Caddesi 150
Dolmabahçe 37, 38, 44, 126, 139
Dolmabahçe Camii 34, 47
Dolmabahçe Sarayı 34, 47, 138
Don Juan 20, 107, 118, 161
Don Quixote 20
Durmuş Dede 59
Dwight, H. G. 58, 65, 69

E

Eğrikapı 90
Eğrikemer 89
Egyptian Embassy 52

174 INDEX

Eirenaion 113
Elena 83
Elias Paşa 136
Eminönü 13
Eminzade Hacı Emin Zade 152
Emirgân 74, 76, 115
Emperor Manuel I Comnenus 148
Emperor Tiberius II 15
Erivan 74
Esma Sultan (1778-1845) 47, 48
Eşek Adası 100
Ethem Pertev Yalısı 116
Eudoxia 94
Eugenie 138
Euphemus 99
Evliya Çelebi (1611-c. 1680) 21, 22, 23, 29, 35, 41, 42, 45, 46, 51, 74, 76, 79, 82, 84, 85, 100, 107, 110, 111, 113, 115, 121, 123, 132, 135, 136, 139, 144, 154, 158,
Evliyalar Tepesi 68
Evmania Voria 146

F

Faik and Bekir Bey Yalısı 79
Fane of Jove 105
Fanum Jovis 101
Fatih 10
Fatih Sultan Mehmet Köprüsü 69, 72, 116
Fener quarter 82
Fenerli Türbe Sokağı 68
Ferid Paşa 72
Fil Burnu 102, 104
Fisherman of Halicarnassus 159
Ford of the Cow 7
French 139
Fromentin 38
Fındıklı 28, 30

G

Galata 15, 18, 19, 35, 79, 82, 85
Galata Köprüsü 11
Galata Tower 15, 18
Gallipoli 85
Garipçe 102
Garipçe Burnu 96, 97
Garwood, David 58
Genoa 80
Genoese 13, 15, 82, 106
Genoese Castle 104
Genoese fortress 91, 112
Georgia 28
Germany 24
Gerome 38
Giant's Grave 107, 110
Glarissa 116
Glaros 115

Glazier Koço 141
Godefroy de Bouillon 84
Gog 29
Göksu 3, 4, 119, 121, 123
Golden Fleece 7, 94, 96
Grand Vezir Kıbrıslı Mehmet Paşa 48
Great Palace of Byzantium 6
Greek Orthodox Church 18
Grosvenor, Edwin A. 67
Güngör Dilmen 140
Güzelce 120
Güzelce Kemer 90
Gyllius, Petrus 1, 5, 6, 8, 10, 11, 35, 52, 76, 89, 90, 93, 96, 97, 98, 101, 102, 104, 105, 106, 108, 109, 110
Gyropolis 96

H

H. Saladin 117
Hacı Mehmet Emin Ağa 34
Hacı Kemalettin 63
Hacı Mehmet Paşa 152
Hacıağzı 104
Hadikat-il Cevami 109, 121
Hafız Ahmet Paşa 26
Hafız Hüseyin Ayvansarayi 108
Haghia Sophia1 60
Halide Edib Adıvar 51
Halil Ethem 34
Halil Paşa 62
Hamlin, Cyrus 55, 68
Harbor of the Ephesians 96
Harpies 96
Hasan Dede 42
Hasan Paşa 85, 86
Hasköy 13
Haydarpaşa Lisesi 157
Hayrettin Paşa 39
Hekimbaşı Salih Efendi Yalısı 116
Hekimoğlu Ali Paşa Çeşmesi 32
Helle 105
Hellenes 6
Hellespont 8, 148
Hendek Sokağı 18
Hera 7, 70
Hermes 105
Hero 148
Herodotus 1, 69, 106
Hezar Para Ahmet Paşa 111
Hızır İlyas 46
Hidiv Kasrı 115
Hieron 94, 106
Hill of the Saints 68
Hisarüstü 68
Histories 1, 69
History of the Ottoman Empire 116
Hittites 88
Homer 7, 8

INDEX

House of Hacı İmer 79
House of Marco Paşa 104
Hünkâr İskelesi 108
Hüseyin Kocabaş 86
Hüseyin Paşa 47, 116, 117
Hüseyin Pektaş 55
Hüsrev Kethüda 46

I

Anatolia 140
Ibrahim the Mad (1640-48) 11
Ihlamur Kasrı 41
Iliad 7
Inachus 7
India 143
International Press Center 11
Io 7
Ionians 8
Iranian 90
Isaac II Angelus (1185-95, 1203-04) 49
Isle of Thynias 101
Istanbul International Community School 67
Istanbul Magazine 139

İ

İbrahim 26, 111, 155
İbrahim Paşa 67, 108
İcadiye Caddesi 141
İhsan Kesedar 63
İmer Faruk Efendi 72
İnciciyan 63
İncirköy 111
İreke Taşı 97
İsa Çelebi 28
İshak Ağa 109
İskele Camii 144
İskender Paşa 116
İskender Paşa Camii 115
İsmail Paşa, the Khedive of Egypt 76
İstinye 76, 78
İznik 88

J

Janissaries 26, 62, 63, 79, 83, 89, 111, 143, 155, 156
Japan 139
Jason 7, 8, 11, 33, 76, 80, 93, 96, 101, 106
Jerusalem 39
Jesuits 17
Jew 125
John V Palaeologus (1341-91) 82
John VI Cantacuzenos (1347-54) 82 94
Joshua 92, 107
Jove 102, 103

Justinian the Great (527-65) 49, 84, 89, 106, 133
Justinian's Aqueduct 90

K

Kabakoz Limanı 100, 102
Kabataş 32, 34
Kadıköy 8, 112, 156
Kağıthane Suyu 5, 90
Kaffa 18
Kaiser Wilhelm II 45, 80
Kale Ağası Sokağı 71
Kalender 80
Kalender Köşkü 80
Kalos Agros 84
Kandilli 128, 131
Kandilli Burnu 128, 131, 132
Kandilli Rasathanesi 132
Kanlıca 115
Kaptan-ı Derya Cezayirli Gazi Hasan Paşa Camii 85
Kapudan Khalil Paşa 79
Karabaş Mescidi 23
Karabaş Mustafa Ağa 23
Karabet Balyan 37
Karaca Ahmet 157
Karacaahmet 157, 158
Karacaahmet Mezarlığı 157
Karaite Jews 13
Karaköy 15
Karataş 93
Kasrı Hümayun 78
Kasım Paşa 86
Kâtip Camii 57
Kavacık Deresi 116
Kavak Burnu 104
Kaya Sultan 43
Kayalar 71
Kayalar Mezarlığı 58, 68
Keçili Liman 104
Keçilik 104
Kefeliköy 84
Kemalettin Bey 52
Kemankeş Caddesi 15, 19
Kemeraltı Caddesi 17
Keroessa 7
Kesedar, İhsan 63
Keys of the Pontus 84, 100
Kıbrıslı Mustafa Emin Paşa 128
Kılıç (the Sword) Ali Paşa 19, 22
Kılıç Ali Paşa Camii 23
Kırmızı (Red) Yalı 130
Kız Kulesi 148
Kilyos 91
Kireçburnu, 83
Kitabı Bahriye 41
Kledai tou Pontou 84, 100
Klistos Limin 11
Knights of the First Crusade 84
Koca Defterdar Paşa 84

INDEX

Koca Yusuf Paşa 32
Köprülü Yalısı 117
Kortel Korusu 52
Köse Mustafa Paşa 17
Kösem 155
Kule Bahçesi 132
Kuleli 156
Kuleli Naval Officers' Training College 133
Kumbaba 113
Kuruçeşme 49, 51
Kuzgun Baba 139
Kuzguncuk 139, 140, 141
Kuzguncuk Camii 140
Küçük Bebek 52
Küçük Esma Sultan 47
Küçüksu 3, 4, 123, 128
Küçüksu Çeşmesi 126
Küçüksu Kasrı 126
Kütahya 88, 108

L

Lale Devri 41
Lale Sera (Tulip Conservatory) 44
Latin knights 10
Lazarists 17
Leander 148
Lechavalier 110
Leda 109
Lemnos 85
Lepanto 19
Levent 78
Locations, Byzantine Chalcedon 142; Chrysokeramos 135; Chrysopolis 142; Diplokion 39; Eirenaion 113; Glaros 115; Kalos Agros 84; Klistos Limin 11; Neapolis 79; Pharmakeus 80; Scutari 142, 143, 158; Stavros 135, 136; Stenos 7
Locations, coastal features: Acar Burnu 108; Akıntı Burnu 51, 52; Akri Psomion 101; Altınkum 96; Ampelodes 102; Anadolufeneri Burnu 102; Anadolukavağı 105, 106, 107, 108; Arm of St. George 148; Asian Cyanean Rock 70, 102; Büyükdere Limanı 84; Büyükliman 96; Çakal Limanı 102; Çayırbaşı 85, 88; Clashing Rocks 97, 100; Coracium 102; Cyanean Rocks 97; Defterdar Burnu 49; Dios Sacra 101; Eşek Adası 101; Fanum Jovis 101; Fil Burnu 102; Garipçe 102; Garipçe Burnu 96, 97; Giant's Grave 107; Hacıağzı 104; İreke Taşı 97; Isle of Thynias 101; Kabakoz Limanı 100, 102; Kandilli Burnu 128, 131, 132; Kavak Burnu 104; Keçili Liman 104; Keçilik 104; Keys of the Pontus 84, 100; Kireçburnu, 83; Kledai tou Pontou 84, 100; Kız Kulesi 148; Macar Bay 108; Mesar Burnu 90; Phrixos 115, 116; Poyraz Bay 102; Poyraz Burnu 102; Promontorium Ancyraenum 101; Promontorium Coracium 101; Quarantine Station 104; Rooky 104; Salacak 148, 150; Sarayburnu 6, 8, 11, 13, 15, 142; Selvi Burnu 108; Symplegades 98; Tahaffuzhane 104; Tellibaba Burnu 91; Xenophon's Cave 113; Yum Burnu 100, 101, 102
Locations, forests: Arifi Paşa Korusu 57; Belgrade Forest 88, 89; Kortel Korusu 52
Locations, Greek: Ajantion 32, 33; Anaplous 49; Argyropolis 30, 32; Calpe 112, 113; Chrysoplis 30; City of Gold 30; City of Silver 30; Comarodes 79 Hieron 94, 106; Neorion 11; Prosphorean Haven 11; Semistra 7; Serapion 94; Sosthenion 76; Therapeia 80, 82; Two Columns 39
Locations, hills and mountains: Aşiyan 58, 59; Alemdağ 122; Bed of Hercules 107; Büyük Çamlıca 4, 160, 162; Çamlıca 161; Mount Bulgurlu 160; Uludağ 160; Yoros Tepesi 105, 106; Yuşa Tepesi 4, 107, 108
Locations, streets: Aşiyan road 71; Ahmet Ağa Sokağı 71; Çinili Cami Sokağı 155; Doğancılar Caddesi 150; Fenerli Türbe Sokağı 68; Hendek Sokağı 18; Kale Ağası Sokağı 71; Kemankeş Caddesi 15, 19; Kemeraltı Caddesi 17; Necatibey Caddesi 19, 23, 28, 30; Rıhtım Caddesi 15; Sahil Yolu 148; Selimiye İskele Caddesi 156; Tophane İskele Caddesi 19; Toptaşı Caddesi 152; Valide İmareti Sokağı 152, 155; İcadiye Caddesi 141; Yuşa Tepesi Yolu 107
Locations, towns and neighborhoods: Albanian Village 51; Anadolufeneri 100; Anadoluhisarı 62, 117, 123; Anadolukavağı 93, 94, 104; Arnavutköy 51, 132; Ayvalık 85; Baltalimanı 72; Beşiktaş 38, 39, 41 42; Bebek 51, 55, 58, 71, 72; Belgrade 88; Beykoz 108, 109, 110, 111; Beylerbeyi 1, 135, 136; Büyükdere 84, 85, 86, 89, 90; City of Gold 142, 162; Çayırbaşı 85, 88; Çengelköy 135; Çubuklu 113, 115; Dolmabahçe 35, 37, 38, 44; Eğrikapı 90; Eminönü 13; Emirgân 74, 76, 115; Fener quarter 82; Fındıklı 28, 30; Galata 15, 18, 19, 35, 79, 82, 85; Hasköy 13; Hisarüstü 68; İncirköy 111; İstinye 76, 78; Kabataş 32, 34; Kadıköy 8, 142, 156; Kandilli 128; Kanlıca 115; Karaköy 15; Kefeliköy 76; Küçük Bebek 52; Küçüksu 123, 128; Kuleli 156; Kumbaba 113; Kuruçeşme 49, 51; Kütahya 78; Kuzguncuk 139, 140, 141; Levent 78; Moanoğlu 136; Ortaköy 1, 46, 47, 48, 49; Paşabahçe 111, 112, 113; Polonezköy 112; Rumelihisarı 58, 59, 63, 65, 67, 68; Rumelikavağı 55, 92, 93, 94, 96, 105; Sarıyer 90; Serapion 105; Stavros 135; Sulukule 86; Şile 112; Taksim Square 89; Tarabya 80, 82, 8 Tellibaba Burnu 92; Tophane 15, 19, 20, 27, 28; Üsküdar 32, 55, 133, 139, 142, 143, 144, 148, 152, 156, 157, 160, 162; Vaniköy 132, 133; Yalıköy 108; Yeniköy 79, 80, 83; Yenimahalle 91; Yıldız 37, 44

INDEX

Lodos 3
Long Aqueduct 89
lost souls 93
Loti, Pierre 117, 130
Lygos 9

M

Mabeyni Hümayun 78
Macar Bay 108
Maglova Kemeri 90
Magog 29
Mahmut I (1730-54) 23, 32, 63, 67, 89
Mahmut II (1808-39) 27, 37, 48, 78, 89, 108, 136, 156
Maiyet Köşkü 41
Malta Köşkü 44
Mandrocles 70
Mandrocles of Samos 1, 69
Manuel I Comnenus 148
Manuk Azaryan Efendi 86
Marco Paşa 104
Marlowe 120
Mary Montagu 161
Maslak Kasrı 78
Mavromoliotissa 94
Mecca 21, 32, 144, 158
Mecidiye Camii 44, 47
Medea 80, 106
Medina 144
Mediterranean 6
Megara 9, 33
Megarians 90
Mehmet 62, 139
Mehmet Ağa 29
Mehmet Ali 108
Mehmet II (1451-81) 10, 23, 24, 26, 35, 68, 94, 107, 120, 121, 135, 139
Mehmet IV (1648-87) 13, 146, 156
Mehmet Köprülü the Cruel 116
Mehmet Paşa 135, 148
Mehmet Tahir Ağa 136
Mehmet the Conqueror 63, 108
Mehmet VI Vahdettin (1918-22) 72
Melek Ahmet Paşa 28, 43
Melek Hanım 48
Melie 109
Merasim Köşkü 41
Mermer (Marble) Köşk 139
Mesar Burnu 90
Mesnevi 42
Metanoia 133
Mevlevi 41
Miguel Cervantes 19
Mihrişah Emine 150
Mihrişah Sultan 43
Mihrimah Sultan 144
Miletos 8
Military Museum in Harbiye 26

Mimar Sinan University 30
Moanoğlu 136
Moldavia 83
Molla Çelebi Camii 32
Molla of Trebizond 79
Mongol horde 120
Monnier 94, 105
Montagu, Edward 89
Montagu, Lady Mary Wortley 88, 161
mosque in Anadoluhisarı 121
Mosque of Victory 27
Mount Bulgurlu 160
Mount of Joshua 107
Mount Olympus of Bithynia 160
Murat I 68
Murat III (1574-95) 20, 111, 132, 135, 154
Murat IV (1623-1640) 17, 43, 67, 74, 132, 155
Murat V 43
Mustafa 29
Mustafa Efendi 57
Mustafa Emin Paşa 130
Mustafa I (1617-18, 1622-23) 155
Mustafa II (1695-1703) 116, 117, 146
Mustafa III (1757-74) 57, 96, 150
Mustafa IV (1807-08) 48
Mustafa Reşit Paşa 72
Mustafa the Virtuous 116
Mycenaean 9, 88
Mycenaeans 9
Myth and legend: Agamemnon 32, 96, 106; Aias 32; Ajax 32; Amycus 76, 109, 110; Apollo 9, 98; Areetes 105, 106; Ares 106; Argo 97, 98, 99, 100, 101; Argos 33; Argonauts 11, 76, 93, 96, 97, 101, 110; Athamas of Boeotia 105; Athena 98, 99; Bebryces 76, 109, 110; Belisarius 5; Boreas 96; Byzas 7, 9, 10; Calais 96; Castor 110; Chalkis 33; Charandas 33; Clashing Rocks 96, 101; Colchis 105, 106, 115; Cybele 94; Euphemus 99; Fane of Jove 105; Golden Fleece 7, 96; Harpies 96; Helle 105; Hera 7, 70; Hero 148; Hermes 105; Inachus 7; Io 7; Jason 7, 8, 11, 33, 76, 80, 93, 96, 101, 106; Jove 102, 104; Keroessa 7; Leander 148; Leda 109; Medea 80, 106; Melie 109; Nephele 105; Neptune 102; Odysseus 8; Olympus 100; Orpheus 110; Phineus 98, 101; Phrixos 105, 106, 115; Polydeuces 109, 110; Porphry 5; Poseidon 7, 109; Symplegades 96; Telamon 32; Tiphys 98; Twelve Olympian Gods 94, 105; Zeus 106, 109; Zeus of the Favorable Wind 105, 106; Zeus Ourious 105

N

Nafi Baba 69
Nakşibendi 17
Narrative of Travels 21
National Geographic Magazine 67

INDEX

Nations:
Abaza 28; Amalfians 13; Arab 90; Arabia 143; Armenia 27; Assyrian 88; Bithynia 113; Bithynians 101; Bohemia 139; Bulgars 76; China 139; China Cossacks 79, 83; Crete 146; France 139; French 139; Genoa 80; Genoese 13, 15, 82, 106; Georgia 28; Hellenes 6; Hittites 88; India 143; Ionians 8; Iranians 90; Japan 139; Jew 125; Karaite Jews 13; Megarians 90; Moldavia 83; Mycenaeans 9; Persia 143; Phrygia 94; Phrygian 88; Pisans 13; Republic of Turkey 10; Russians 106; Scoavonia 128; Scythians 1; Turkey 2; Turkish Republic 1; Urartian 88; Venetians 10, 13, 62, 82; Venice 80; Wallachia 83, 125
Naval Museum 40
Neapolis 79
Necatibey Caddesi 19, 23, 28, 30
Nefii Efendi. 37
Neorion 11
Nephele 105
Neptune 102
Nevşehirli Damat İbrahim Paşa 43
New Army 156, 157
New Mosque 13
New Quarter 91
Nişancı Kara Davut Paşa 146
Nicetas Choniates 148
Nicholas I of Montenegro 83
Nicolo Pisani 82
Nightingale, Florence 55, 133, 156, 157
Nizen Dervish Yusuf Jelali 42
Nur Banu 152, 154
Nüshed Baba 69
Nusretiye Camii 27, 34

O

Odysseus 8
Odyssey 8
Old Saray 155
Olympus 100
open-air mosques 121
Orders: Akoimetai 113; Benedictines 17; Jesuits 17; Lazarists 17
Orhan Veli (1914-50) 58
Orloff of Russia 108
Orpheus 110
Ortaköy 1, 46, 47, 48, 49
Osman II (1618-22) 35, 155
Osman Paşa 111
Ostrorog, Jean 130
Ostrorog Yalısı 130
Ottoman fort 98
Ottoman Reform movement 72
Ottoman Turks 10
Our Lady of Comarodes 80
Ovid 91
Ovid's Tower 91

P

Paşabahçe 111, 112, 113
Paşalar Dairesi 78
Palace of Beylerbeyi 138
Palace of Ferid Paşa 72
Palace of İmer Faruk Efendi 72
Palaces of the Sultanas (Istanbul Magazine, 1992) 48
Palaeologues 94, 106
Panayia 17, 18
Panayia Commariotisa 80
Papa Eftim 18
Papa Khalfa 78
Papazkarası 132
Pardoe, Julia 118, 123, 126, 130, 138, 160, 161
Paris 27
Patriarch Atticus (406-25) 30, 80
Patriarch Efthemios I 18
Patriarch Taraise 84
*pazar kayık*s 13
Peace of Carlowitz 117
Peaceful 113
Pektaş, Hüseyin 55
Persia 24, 143
Persons, ancient: Alexander the Great 29; Darius 1, 10; Mandrocles 70; Mandrocles of Samos 1, 69; Xenophon 113
Persons, creative: Ayvasovski 139; Balyan family 44; Balyan, Karabet 37; Balyan, Kirkor 27, 34, 37; Balyan, Nikogos 34, 37, 41, 47, 48, 126; Balyan, Sarkis 48, 108; Nikogos 34, 37, 41, 47, 48, 126; Baron de Tott 102; Bartlett, Charles 160; Byron 161; Cervantes 19; Cevat Şakir Kabaağaçlı 159; Kabaağaçlı 159; D'Aronco, Raimondo 45, 52; Evliya 158; Fishe Raimondo 45, 52; Fisherman of Halicarnassus 159; Güngör Dilmen 140; H.Saladin 117; Hacı Kemalettin 63; Hafız Hüseyin Ayvansarayi 108; Halide Edib Adıvar 51; Hüseyin Kocabaş 86; Hüseyin Pektaş 55; Kemalettin Bey 52; Loti, Pier 130; Mehmet Tahir Ağa 136; Mehmet, Cervantes, Miguel 19; Monnier 94, 105; Nefii Efendi 37; Nightingale, Florence 133, 156, 157; Orhan Veli (1914-50) 58; Ovid 91; Papa Khalfa 78; Piri Reis (1465-1554) 41; Robert, Christopher 55; Sare Teyze 141; Sechan 38; Sinan 19, 21, 22, 29, 39, 40, 45, 46, 47, 89, 115, 144, 147, 152, 154; Takiuddin 132; Tevfik Fikret (1867 - 1915) 58; Toussaint 94, 105; Uryanizade Ahmet Esat Efendi 140; Yahya Kemal Beyatlı (1884-1958) 39; İsa Çelebi 28; Zühdü Müridoğlu 39
Persons, official: Abbas Hilmi Paşa 115; Abdullah Paşa 74; Ahmet Paşa 111; Ahmet Vefik Paşa 67, 68; Ali Paşa 19; Atatürk 37, 38; Atatürk, Kemal 10; Balta Oğlu (Son of the Axe) 72; Barbarossa 39, 40; Bülent Ecevit 57; Çelik Gülersoy 44; Cezayirli Gazi Hasan Paşa 85; Cezayirli Palabıyık 85; Defterdar Paşa 49; Edward

INDEX

Montagu 89; Elias Paşa 136; Eminzade Hacı Emin Zade 152; Evliya 144; Ferid Paşa 72; Godefroy de Bouillon 84; Grand Vezir Kıbrıslı Mehmet Paşa 48; Hacı Mehmet Emin Ağa 34; Hacı Mehmet Paşa 152; Hafız Ahmet Paşa 26; Halil Paşa 62; Hasan Paşa 86; Hayrettin Paşa 39; Hekimoğlu Ali Paşa 32; Hezar Para Ahmet Paşa 111; Hüseyin Paşa 47, 116, 117; Hüsrev Kethüda 46; İbrahim Paşa 67, 108; İshak Ağa 109; İsmail Paşa, the Khedive of Egypt 76; Karabaş Mustafa Ağa 23; Kasım Paşa 86; Koca Defterdar Paşa 84; Koca Yusuf Paşa 32; Köse Mustafa Paşa 17; Kılıç (the Sword) Ali Paşa 19, 22; Manuk Azaryan Efendi 86; Marco Paşa 104; Mehmet Ali 108; Mehmet Paşa 135, 148; Melek Ahmet Paşa 28, 43; Melek Hanım 48; Molla of Trebizond 79; Mustafa Emin Paşa 130; Mustafa Reşit Paşa 72; Nevşehirli Damat İbrahim Paşa 43; Nişancı Kara Davut Paşa 146; Nicolo Pisani 82; Osman Paşa 111; Petek Ali Bey 67; Podesta 15; Rakım Paşa 67; Rıza Kaptan 52; Rüstem Paşa 40, 144; Saruca Paşa 62, 67; Sheikh Heydayi Mehmet 158; Sinan Paşa 40; Sokollu Mehmet Paşa 46, 82, 132; Şemsi Paşa 147; Şerif of Mecca 144; Tophane Müşiri Zeki Paşa 72; Uluç Ali 19; Ypsilantis 83; Zağanos Paşa 62, 63

Persons, religious: Şeyh Kara Şemseddin 113; Abu Sufyan 15; Amiri Wahibi 15; Asumani Dede 158; Celaladin Rumi 42; Durmuş Dede 59; Hamlin, Cyrus 55, 68; Hasan Dede 42; Hızır İlyas 46; Joshua 107; Karaca Ahmet 157; Karacaahmet 157; Kuzgun Baba 139; Nafi Baba 69; Nightingale, Florence 55; Nizen Dervish Yusuf Jelali 42; Nüshed Baba 69; Papa Eftim 18; Patriarch Atticus 80; Patriarch Atticus (406-25) 30; Patriarch Efthemios I 18; Patriarch Taraise 84; Simeon the Stylite 49; Siyavuş Paşa 28; St. Alexander 113; St. Andrew the Apostle 30; St. Stachys 30; Stylite Daniel 49; Telli Baba 91, 92; Vani Efendi 132; Yashka 38; Yuşa 92, 107

Persons, royal: Abdülaziz 38, 42, 48, 72, 80, 138; Abdülhamit I (1774-89) 32; Abdülhamit II (1876-1909) 29, 37, 44, 45, 47, 67, 68, 72, 78, 80, 83, 136, 138; Abdülmecit (1839-61) 34, 37, 38, 41, 44, 47, 72, 112, 126, 156; Adam Czartoryski 112; Ahmet I (1603-17) 35, 155, 158; Ahmet III (1703-30) 41, 47, 144, 146, 152; Ahmet the Statist 116; Anastasia 155; Andronicus I Comnenus (1183-85) 89; Artaxerxes II 113; Baiazeth 120; Beyazit I (1389-1403) 62, 107, 120, 121; Beyazit II (1481-1512) 23, 24, 26, 111, 113; Bezmiâlem Valide Sultan 34; Cihangir 29; Comnenus, Manuel I. (1143-80) 94; Constantine the Great (324-37) 49, 76; Constantine XI (1449-53) 62; Crazy İbrahim 156; Czar Nicholas II 38; Cyrus the Younger 113; Darius 69, 70, 71, 106; Don Juan 20; Elena 83; Emirgüne 74; Esma Sultan (1778-1845) 47, 48; Eudoxia 94; Eugenie 138; Evmania Voria 146; Fatih 10; Ibrahim the Mad (1640-48) 11; İbrahim 26, 111, 155; İmer Faruk Efendi 72; Isaac II Angelus (1185-95, 1203-04) 49; John VI Cantacuzenos 94; John V Palaeologus (1341-91) 82; Justinian the Great (527-65) 49, 84, 89, 106, 133; Kaiser Wilhelm II 45, 80; Kaya Sultan 43; Kösem 155; Küçük Esma Sultan 47; Lightning 120; Mahmut I (1730-54) 23, 32, 63, 67, 89; Mahmut II (1808-39) 27, 37, 48, 78, 89, 108, 136, 156; Manuel I Comnenus 148; Mehmet II (1451-81) 23, 10, 24, 26, 35, 62, 68, 94, 107, 120, 121, 135, 139; Mehmet IV (1648-87) 13, 146, 156; Mehmet Köprülü the Cruel 116; Mehmet the Conqueror 63, 108; Mehmet VI Vahdettin (1918-22) 72; Mihrişah Emine 150; Mihrişah Sultan 43; Mihrimah Sultan 144; Murat I [1359-89] 83, 68; Murat III (1574-95) 20, 111, 132, 135, 136, 154; Murat IV (1623-1640) 17, 43, 67, 74, 79, 132, 155; Murat V 43; Mustafa 29; Mustafa Efendi 57; Mustafa I (1617-18, 1622-23) 155; Mustafa II (1695-1703) 116, 117, 146; Mustafa III (1757-74) 57, 96, 150; Mustafa IV (1807-08) 48; Mustafa the Virtuous 116; Nicholas I of Montenegro 83; Nur Banu 152, 154; Orloff of Russia 108; Osman II (1618-22) 35, 155; Ostrorog, Jean 130; Prusias of Bithynia 106; Rabia Gülnus Emetullah 146; Romanus I Lecapenus 76; Romanus II Lecapenus (919-44) 39; Rose of Spring 146; Sabiha Sultan 72; Selim I (1512-20) 35, 84, 113, 115, 132, 154, 158; Selim II (1566-74) 19, 48, 84, 152; Selim III (1789-1807) 26, 43, 83, 126, 133, 156, 157; Selim the Sot 154; Septimius Severus 106; Süleyman I 26, 29, 39, 40; Süleyman I 23, 26; Süleyman the Magnificent (1520-66) 23, 29, 45, 79, 88, 89, 108, 132, 144; Tamurlane 120; Theodora 133; Tiberius II (578-82) 15; Tulip King 41, 144; Turhan Hatice 13, 156; Tzar Symeon 76; Valide Sultan 13; Valide Sultan Mihrişah 126; Victor Emmanuel III of Italy 83; Yahya Efendi 45, 46; Yıldırım 120

Pertek Ali Bey 67
Pharmakeus 80
Phineaus 96
Phineus 97, 98, 101
Phrixos 105, 106, 115, 116
Phrygia 94
Phrygian 88
Piri Reis (1465-1554) 41
Pisani, Nicolo 82
Pisans 13
Podesta 15
Polonezköy 112
Polydeuces 109, 110
Pompey's Column 98
Poplar Point 104

Poseidon 109
Poyraz Bay 102
Poyraz Burnu 102
Presidential Palace 80
Procopius 133, 162
Promontorium Ancyraeum 101
Promontorium Coracium 101
Promontorium Simas 90
Prosphorean Haven 11
Prusias of Bithynia 106
Pyrgos 89
Pythian Odes 8

Q

Quarantine Station 104

R

Rabia Gülnus 146
Rabia Gülnus Emetullah 146
Rakım Paşa 67
Rasim Paşa Yalısı 115
Regions: Anadolu 1, 2; Arabia 24; Bithynia 112; Bulgaria 2; Germany 24; Gog 29; Magog 29; Persia 24; Rumeli 1, 2, 135; Syria 108; Thessalonika 138; Thrace 2, 7; Venetians 24
Repentance 133, 135
Republic of Turkey 10
Resim ve Heykel Müzesi 41
Rethymnon 146
Rhebas 101
Riva Deresi 100
Rivers: Alibey Suyu 5, 90; Chryso Keras 5; Cidaris 90; Glarissa 116; Göksu 3, 4, 119, 121, 123; Kâğıthane Suyu 5, 90; Kavacık Deresi 116; Küçüksu 3, 4; Rhebas 101; Riva Deresi 101; Sweet Waters of Asia 3, 4, 119, 123, 132; Sweet Waters of Europe 5, 90
Rıza Kaptan 52
Robert, Christopher 55
Robert College 51, 55, 57, 65, 68
Robert College Community School 67
Romanus I Lecapenus 76
Romanus II Lecapenus (919-44) 39
Romanus IV Diogenes (1067-81) 94
Rome 2, 10
Rooky 104
Rose of Spring 146
Rule of Women 154
Rum 2
Rum Mehmet Paşa Camii 148, 150
Rumeli 1, 2, 135
Rumelifeneri 2, 97, 100
Rumelihisarı 1, 2, 49, 55, 57, 58, 59, 63, 65, 67, 68, 71, 72, 106, 119, 120
Rumelikavağı 55, 92, 93, 94, 96, 105

Russians 106
Rüstem Paşa 40, 144
Rıhtım Caddesi 15

S

Sabancı mansion 76
Sabiha Sultan 72
Sadberk Hanım Museum 86
Sadullah Paşa Yalısı 135
Sahil Yolu 148
Salacak 148, 150
Saladin, H. 117
Salamis 32
Samos 71
Sarayburnu 6, 8, 11, 13, 15, 142
Sardis 113
Sare Teyze 141
Sarkis Balyan 48, 108, 138
Saruca Paşa 62, 67
Sarı (Yellow) Köşk 139
Sarıyer 90
Sclavonia 128
Scutari 142, 143, 158
Scutarion 150
Scythians 1
Sechan 38
Secret History 133
Selim I (1512-20) 35, 84, 113, 115, 132, 154, 158
Selim II (1566-74) 19, 48, 84, 152
Selim III (1789-1807) 26, 43, 83, 126, 133, 156, 157
Selim the Sot 154
Selimiye barracks 133, 156, 157
Selimiye Camii 157
Selimiye İskele Caddesi 156
Selvi Burnu 108
Semistra 7
Semitic 2
Sepetçiler Kasrı 11, 13
Septimius Severus 106
Serai Bournou 160
Serapion 94, 106
Seven Towers 161
Seyahatname 21, 22, 23, 28, 143
Sheikh Hedayi Mehmet 158
Simeon the Stylite 49
Sinan 19, 21, 22, 29, 39, 40, 45, 46, 47, 89, 90, 115, 144, 147, 152, 154
Sinop 8
Sinope 8
Siyavuş Paşa 28
Society of the Friends of Istanbul 117
Sokollu Mehmet Paşa 46, 82, 132
Something's Up! 58
Sosthenion 76
Sources: Aelian 52; *Anabasis* 112; Apollonius 98, 109, 110; Appollonius of Rhodes 7, 97; *Argonautica* 7. 97, 98, 109; Aziyade 130; *Book of the Sea* 41; Byron 107, 118, 161;

Çelebi 28; Cengiz Bektaş 139, 140; Cervantes 19; Cicero 106; *Constantinople, Settings and Traits* 58; Desenchantees 130; Dionysius Byzantius 52, 98, 110; *Don Juan* 107, 118, 161; *Don Quixote* 20; Quixote 20; Dwight, H. G. 58, 65, 69; Edifices 162; Evliya Çelebi (1611- c.1680) 21, 22, 23, 29, 35, 38, 41, 42, 45, 46, 51, 74, 76, 79, 82, 84, 85, 100, 107, 110, 111, 113, 115, 121, 123, 132, 135, 136, 139, 143, 154, 158, 162; ; *Gardens of the Mosques* 109; Garwood, David 58; Grosvenor, Edwin A. 67; Gyllius 5, 6, 8, 9, 10, 11, 35, 52, 76, 89, 90, 93, 96, 97, 98, 101, 104, 105, 106, 108, 109, 110; Gyllius, Petrus 1; Hadikat 121; *Hadikat-il Cevami* 109; Hafız Hüseyin Ayvansarayi 108, 121; Halil Ethem 34; Herodotus 1, 69, 106; *Histories* 1, 69; history of the Emperor's wars 162; *History of the Ottoman Empire* 116; Homer 7, 8; *Iliad* 7; Istanbul Magazine 139; Josef von Hammer 22, 116; Kandilli 131; *Kitabı Bahriye* 41; Lechavalier 110; *March Up-Country* 112; Marlowe 120; Melek Hanım 48; Montagu, Lady Mary Wortley 88, 161; *Narrative of Travels* 21; Nicetas Choniates 148; *Odyssey* 8; *Palaces of the Sultanas* (Istanbul Magazine, 1992) 48; 1992) 48; Pardoe, Julia 123, 126, 130, 138, 160, 161; Phineus 97; Pindar 8; Pliny 97; Procopius 133, 162; *Pythian Odes* 8; *Secret History* 133; *Seyahatname* 21, 22, 23, 28, 143; *Something's Up!* 58; Tamburlaine 120; *The Beauties of the Bosphorus* 118, 123, 126, 130, 160; Tülay Artan 48; Xenophon 112; İhsan Kesedar 63; İnciciyan 63
Spanish Chapel 86
St. Alexander 29, 113
St. Andrew the Apostle 30
St. Benoit 17
St. George 79
St. George of the Mangana 148
St. Gregory at Etchmiadzin 17
St. Gregory the Illuminator 17
St. John of Studius 113
St. John the Baptist 17
St. Nicholas 17
St. Sophia 160
St. Stachys 30
St. Theodore of Tiron 84
Stavros 135, 136
Stenos 76
stin poli 6
Straits: Boğaziçi 11; Dardanelles 3; Ford of the Cow 7; Hellespont 8, 148
Strange Cape 96
Street of the Moat 18
Stylite Daniel 49
Sublime Porte 108
Süleyman 19, 26, 29, 39, 40
Süleyman I 23, 26
Süleyman the Magnificent (1520-66) 23, 29, 45, 79, 88, 89, 108, 115, 132, 144
Sultaniye Deresi 111
Sulukule 86
Sumner-Boyd, Hilary 39
Surp Kirkor Lusavoriç 17, 140
Sürre-i-Hümayun 143, 144
Susa 70
Sweet Waters of Asia 3, 4, 119, 123, 132
Sweet Waters of Europe 5, 90
Symeon, Tzar 76
Symplegades 96, 98
Syria 108

Ş

Şale Köşkü 44, 45
Şehitlik 68
Şemsi Paşa 147
Şemsi Paşa Camii 147, 148
Şerif of Mecca 144
Şerifler Yalısı 74
Şeyh Kara Şemseddin 113
Şile 112

T

Tahaffuzhane 104
Takiuddin 132
Taksim Square 89
Tamburlaine 120
Tamurlane 120
Tanzimat 72
Tarabya 80, 82, 89
Tarabya Greek Orthodox church 82
Taxiarchs 51
Telamon 32
Telli Baba 91, 92
Tellibaba Burnu 91, 92
temple of Dionysus 70
Tevfik Fikret (1867-1915) 58
The Beauties of the Bosphorus 118, 123, 126, 130 , 160
Theodora 133
Theodosian walls 6, 86
Therapeia 80, 82
Thessalonika 138
Thrace 2, 7
Tiberius II (578-82) 15
Tinos 155
Tiphys 98
Tokat Deresi 108
Tomi 91
Tophane 15, 19, 20, 23, 27, 28, 29
Tophane Çeşmesi 23
Tophane Müşiri Zeki Paşa 72
Tophane İskele Caddesi 19
Topkapı Sarayı 6, 13, 37, 146, 154, 155, 160
Toptaşı Caddesi 152

INDEX

Toussaint 94, 105
Treaty of Baltalimanı 72
Trebizond 79, 113
Tripoli 39
Trojan War 7
Troy 32
Tulip Festivals 41
Tulip King 41, 144
Tunis 20, 39, 40
Turhan Hatice 13, 156
Turkish Maritime Lines 15, 19
Turkish Orthodox Church 18
Tzar Symeon 76

U

Uluç Ali 19
Uludağ 160
Umar sand banks 108
Urartian 88
Uryanizade Ahmet Esat Efendi 140
Uryanizade Camii 140
Uzunkemer 89

Ü

Üsküdar 32, 55, 133, 139, 142, 143, 144, 148, 152, 156, 157, 160, 162

V

Valide Sultan 13
Valide Sultan Mihrişah 126
Valide İmareti Sokağı 152, 155
Vani Efendi 132
Vaniköy 132, 133
Varna 91
Veli, Orhan (1914-50) 58
Venetians 10, 13, 24, 82
Victor Emmanuel III of Italy 83
Virgin Hodeghetria 18
von Hammer, Joseph 22, 116

W

Wallachia 83, 125

Whirling Dervishes 41
Wired-up Saint 92

X

Xenophon 112, 113
Xenophon's Cave 113

Y

Yahya Efendi 45, 46
Yahya Kemal Beyatlı (1884-1958) 39
Yalıköy 108
Yashka 38
Yeşil Sera (Green Conservatory) 44
Yeni Cami 13
Yeni Valide Camii 146
Yeniköy 79, 80, 83
Yenimahalle 91
Yeraltı Camii 15
Yıldız 37, 44
Yıldız Parkı 43, 44
Yıldız Sarayı 43, 44
Yoros 93
Yoros Tepesi 105, 106
Ypsilantis 83
Yuşa 92, 107
Yuşa Tepesi 4, 107, 108
Yuşa Tepesi Yolu 107
Yum Burnu 100, 101, 102
Yılanlı Yalı 57, 58
Yıldırım 120
Yıldız Sarayı 139

Z

Zağanos Paşa 62, 63
Zaim Mustafa Paşa Yalısı 117
Zetes 96
Zeus 7, 106, 109
Zeus of the Favorable Wind 106
Zeus of the Favoring Wind 105
Zeus Ourious 105, 106
Zonaro 38
Zühdü Müridoğlu 39